C. P. E.

Unlocking the Masters Series, No. 28

Series Editor: Robert Levine

C. P. E.

A Listener's Guide to the Other Bach

David Hurwitz

AMADEUS PRESS
An Imprint of Hal Leonard Corporation

Published in 2016 by Amadeus Press
An Imprint of Hal Leonard Corporation
7777 West Bluemound Road
Milwaukee, WI 53213

Trade Book Division Editorial Offices
33 Plymouth St., Montclair, NJ 07042

Printed in the United States of America

Book design by Snow Creative

Library of Congress Cataloging-in-Publication Data

Names: Hurwitz, David, 1961– author.
Title: C. P. E. : a listener's guide to the other Bach / David Hurwitz.
Other titles: Carl Philipp Emanuel
Description: Montclair, NJ : Amadeus Press, 2016. | Series: Unlocking the masters series ; 28 | Includes bibliographical references.
Identifiers: LCCN 2016010122 | ISBN 9781574674675 (pbk.)
Subjects: LCSH: Bach, Carl Philipp Emanuel, 1714–1788—Criticism and interpretation.
Classification: LCC ML410.B16 H87 2016 | DDC 780.92—dc23
LC record available at http://lccn.loc.gov/2016010122

www.amadeuspress.com

To Styra Avins

Contents

Acknowledgments

This book would not have been possible without the kind help and encouragement of Paul Corneilson, managing editor of the C. P. E. Bach Complete Works, published under the auspices of the Packard Humanities Institute. In fact, he deserves the gratitude of music lovers everywhere, as do the remarkable group of scholars engaged in work on the Edition, names such as the late Christopher Hogwood, Christoph Wolff, Robert D. Levin, Peter Wollny, Darrell Berg, Ulrich Leisinger, and all of the contributors to the individual volumes. The work of musicologists often seems remote from our daily lives and seldom gets noticed, but their achievements combine brilliance, sweat, tears, and an endless concern for detail without which C. P. E. Bach's music could not be revived. We are so much the richer for their efforts.

I also wish to thank the friends and family without whose support my work would not have been possible: my parents, brother Dan and sister Jodie, Styra Avins, Sylvia Kahan, David Vernier, Sören Meyer-Eller, Christophe Huss, and my editor Bob Levine. To the folks at Amadeus Press, publisher John Cerullo especially, I am deeply grateful for their willingness to take a risk on C. P. E. Despite my own enthusiasm about his (to my ears) self-evident greatness, he is still not a household word and books about serious classical music remain what we call, euphemistically, a "niche market." If Bach's music emerges, even slightly, from that niche as a result of this book, we have them to thank.

C. P. E. Bach Timeline

Date	C. P. E. Bach Life and Work	Contemporary Works/Events
1714	Born in Weimar	Vivaldi: "La stravaganza" (12 Violin Concertos); birth of Gluck
1731	First publication (Minuet in C Major, Wq 111); first sonatas composed	J. S. Bach: Orchestral Suite No. 3 BWV 1068
1732	Sonatas, Wq 65, 2 & 3	Birth of Haydn
1733	Keyboard Concerto in A Minor, Wq 1	Rameau: *Hippolyte et Aricie*; Telemann: *Tafelmusik* (Table Music)
1734	Six Sonatinas, Wq 64, 1–6	Handel: 6 Concerti Grossi Op. 3
1738	Joins the retinue of Crown Prince Frederick as keyboard accompanist	J. S. Bach: Harpsichord Concertos Nos. 1–7 (BWV 1052–58); Domenico Scarlatti: 30 Sonatas (*Essercizi*) published
1740	Appointed court harpsichordist in Berlin to King Frederick [the Great]	G. B. Sammartini: Early Symphonies; Zelenka: Missa Dei Patris
1741	Symphony in G Major, Wq 173; Keyboard Concerto in A Major, Wq 8	J. S. Bach: Goldberg Variations published; Rameau: *Pièces de Clavecin en Concert*
1742	Six "Prussian" Sonatas	Handel: *Messiah*
1743	Six "Württemberg" Sonatas	Birth of Luigi Boccherini
1744	Keyboard Concerto, Wq 11, published	J. S. Bach: *The Well-Tempered Clavier* (II)
1745	Concertos, Wq 15–18; various sonatas	Rameau: *Platée*
1749	Magnificat (first version)	Handel: *Royal Fireworks Music*

continued

Date	C. P. E. Bach Life and Work	Contemporary Works/Events
1750	Various sonatas and concertos; "Trinklied" (Drinking Song), Wq 199/5	J. S. Bach: *The Art of Fugue* published; J.S. Bach dies; birth of Antonio Salieri
1751	Two Trios, Wq 161, published	Francesco Geminiani: *The Art of Playing on the Violin* published
1752	Keyboard Concerto, Wq 25, published	Handel: *Jephtha*
1753	*Essay on the True Art of Playing the Keyboard* published; Six *Probestücke* (Practice Pieces), Wq 63, 1–6, published	W. F. Bach: Sinfonia in D Major, Fk 64; Rousseau: *Le Devin du village* (first public performance)
1755	Symphonies, Wq 174–176	Gluck: *La danza; L'innocenza giustificata*
1756	Character Pieces, Wq 117	Birth of W. A. Mozart; Leopold Mozart: *Violin School* published
1757	Sonatas, Wq 62, 16–20	Haydn: First String Quartets; Scarlatti dies
1758	Twelve Little Pieces (I), Wq 181, published; Gellert Songs, Wq 194, published	Johann Stamitz: Orchestral Trios Op. 4 published
1759	Sonatas, Wq 50, 1–4,6	Haydn: Symphony No. 1; Handel dies
1760	Sonatas with Varied Reprises, Wq 50, published; Keyboard Concerto, Wq 14, published; Keyboard Concertos, Wq 18, 24, 34, published (in London)	J. C. Bach: *Artaserse*; Boccherini: Six String Trios Op. 1; Niccolò Piccini: *La buona figliuola*; Birth of Luigi Cherubini
1761	*Fortsetzung* (Sequel) of Six Sonatas, Wq 51, published	Gluck: *Don Juan* (ballet); Boccherini: String Quartets Op. 2; Haydn: Symphonies Nos. 6–8 ("Le Matin," "Le Midi," "Le Soir")

continued

Date	C. P. E. Bach Life and Work	Contemporary Works/Events
1762	*Essay on the True Art of Keyboard Playing*, Part II published; Odes, Wq 199, published	Gluck: *Orfeo ed Euridice*; Hasse: *Il trionfo di Clelia*; Franz Ignaz Beck: Six Symphonies Op. 2
1763	2nd Sequel (*Zweyte Fortsetzung*) of Six Sonatas, Wq 52, published	Gluck: *Ezio* (second version)
1765	*Clavierstücke verschiedener Art* (Keyboard Pieces in Different Styles), Wq 112, published	Haydn: Symphony No. 31 "Hornsignal"; W. F. Bach: 12 Polonaises
1766	*Kurze und leichte Clavierstücke* (Short and Easy Keyboard Pieces), Wq 113, published	Carl Joseph Toeschi: *Mars et Vénus* J. C. Bach: Six Sonatas Op. 5
1767	*Kurze und leichte Clavierstücke* II, Wq 114	Gluck: *Alceste*; Telemann dies
1768	Moves to Hamburg as music director of the principal churches; *Kurze und leichte Clavierstücke* II, Wq 114, published	Christian Cannabich: *Renaud et Armide*; Dittersdorf: National Symphony in the Style of Five Nations
1769	*Die Israeliten in der Wüste* (The Israelites in the Desert), Wq 238 (oratorio)	Haydn: String Quartets Op. 9
1770	*Passions-Cantate*, Wq 233; *Damensonaten* (Sonatas for Ladies), Wq 54, published	Birth of Beethoven
1771	Inauguration Music H 821B/C	Boccherini: Six Symphonies Op. 12
1772	Six Concertos, Wq 43, published	Haydn: String Quartets Op. 20; "Farewell" Symphony; Salieri: *La secchia rapita*
1773	Six Symphonies for strings, Wq 182	Mozart: Symphony No. 25, K. 183

continued

Date	C. P. E. Bach Life and Work	Contemporary Works/Events
1774	*Auferstehung und Himmelfahrt Jesu* (Resurrection and Assumption of Jesus), Wq 240; Cramer/Psalms, Wq 196, published	Boccherini: String Quintets Op. 18 Haydn: Symphony No. 60 "Il Distratto"
1776	Accompanied Sonatas I, Wq 90 & II, Wq 89, published	Haydn: Piano Sonatas, Hob. 27–31; F. J. Gossec: *Symphonie de chasse*
1777	Accompanied Sonatas III, Wq 91, published	Mozart: Piano Concerto No. 9, K. 271; J. C. Bach: Six Sonatas Op. 17
1779	*Heilig ist Gott* (Sanctus), Wq 217, published; *Kenner und Liebhaber* (Connoisseurs and Amateurs) Collection I, Wq 55, published	Gluck: *Iphigénie en Tauride*; Cherubini: *Il Quinto Fabio*
1780	*Kenner und Liebhaber* II, Wq 56, published; Orchestral Symphonies, Wq 183, published	Mozart: *Vesperae solennes de confessore* in C Major, K. 339
1781	*Kenner und Liebhaber* III, Wq 57, published	Haydn: String Quartets Op. 33
1782	Fantasias, Wq 58, 6 & 7;, Wq 59, 5	Mozart: *Die Entführung aus dem Seraglio*; Boccherini: Six Symphonies Op. 35
1783	*Kenner und Liebhaber* IV, Wq 58, published	Mozart: "Haydn" Quartets
1784	*Morgengesang, Wq* 239 published	Salieri: *Les Danaïdes*
1785	*Kenner und Liebhaber* V, Wq 59, published	Haydn: Paris Symphonies
1786	Two Litanies, Wq 204, published	Mozart: *Le Nozze di Figaro*; Birth of Carl Maria von Weber

continued

Date	C. P. E. Bach Life and Work	Contemporary Works/Events
1787	*Kenner und Liebhaber* VI, Wq 61, published; Six New Sonatinas, Wq 63, 7–12, published	Mozart: *Don Giovanni*; Gluck dies; Haydn: *The Seven Last Words* published
1788	3 Quartets, Wq 93–95; Concerto for Harpsichord and Fortepiano; C. P. E. Bach dies on December 14	Haydn: String Quartets Op. 54/55; Mozart: Symphonies Nos. 39–41

Introduction

Navigating Through C. P. E. Bach

The posthumous reputation of any very prolific composer depends in large degree on the work of scholars and publishers. This is especially true of C. P. E. Bach, whose output consists primarily of a huge corpus of pieces simply called *sonata*, which can easily take on the appearance of a faceless mountain of similar-looking material absent some overriding organizational principle. The existence of a reliable catalog of works permits listeners to explore the music in manageable chunks, locating and remembering favorite pieces, but even before listeners and (today) record collectors have that opportunity, scholars need to be able to identify and describe the music so that performers can play and record it. It's safe to say that composers such as Mozart, with his "K" numbers (for Köchel) or Schubert with his "D" numbers (for Deutsch) would have been much slower to acquire their current reputations had not good catalogs of works been available to guide the discovery and dissemination of their music.

The situation with C. P. E. Bach is particularly galling because he was a singularly tidy and well-organized composer. He kept his own working catalog that was, for its time, extremely accurate, and this became the basis, after his death in 1788, for the so-called *Nachlass Verzeichnis*, or "Estate Catalog" put together by his wife and daughter and published in 1790. This book not only contained a very complete résumé of all of Bach's most important works, it also listed his holdings of music by other composers, his musical instruments, and his vast and amazingly comprehensive portrait collection of famous musicians. In short, there never has been much doubt about what Bach wrote, and since he made a living publishing his own music in personally supervised, very neat and clean editions, much of his most important production exists (or existed) in print. This still left plenty of music in manuscript, arrangements of pieces by other hands both known and anonymous, and a goodly quantity of dubious attributions, but the main outlines of his achievement always have been gratifyingly clear.

For much of the nineteenth century, however, this material might not have existed. The published works were out of print or unavailable, manuscripts moldered away in the basements of libraries and sat, inaccessible, in private collections, and the ever-increasing importance of organizing and printing the work of his father—the great Johann Sebastian Bach—almost none of which had been catalogued or published at all, reduced poor Carl Philipp Emanuel to the status of a historical footnote. He became a "historically interesting" name rather than a lynchpin of the active repertoire. We will explore this phenomenon in greater depth in the first chapter, but for our purposes now what matters is the fact that no one took on the task of identifying and organizing C. P. E.'s legacy until the Belgian scholar Alfred Wotquenne published his thematic catalog in 1905, over a century after his subject's death. Ever since, most of Bach's works have been graced with a "Wq" number, and Wotquenne's catalog remains the standard to this day.

However, it is not the only standard. In 1989 E. Eugene Helm published a new, more complete catalog of his own, including many works excluded by Wotquenne. The difference between the two can be summarized neatly by the fact that Wotquenne's catalog contains about 279 items, while Helm's offers around 874. How is this possible? Well, Wotquenne respected Bach's published collections, and organized the miscellaneous manuscripts and most individually published pieces similarly, so a single "Wq" number might contain anywhere from two to fifty or more individual works. Thus, Bach's collection of six "Prussian" Sonatas comprises Wq 48, and within Wq 48 they are numbered 1–6; so, if you see Wq 48/4, it means the fourth sonata in that particular collection. This proved to be a convenient and easily digestible method of grouping and identifying a very large number of single works. Helm, on the other hand, most of the time assigns a separate number to each piece individually and, in theory, chronologically (he makes an exception and follows Wotquenne's system for song collections and the like). His catalog has the benefit of more modern scholarship and it is, strictly speaking, more accurate, but also more unwieldy simply on account of its greater size.

Making matters even more confusing, Wotquenne and Helm begin at different points, and therefore their numbering systems do not even correspond in the broadest sense. Let me explain. Most musical catalogs, chronological or not, are organized by genre: orchestral music and its subgenres (such as symphonies and concertos), chamber music (solo sonatas, duets, trios, and quartets), vocal music (choral works, operas, and songs), and so forth. Both Wotquenne and Helm adopt this convention. However, Wotquenne has as his "Wq 1" a concerto, whereas Helm begins with the solo keyboard works. This makes sense since Bach's first printed piece is a tiny minuet for harpsichord. So, the piece listed as H 1 in Helm's catalog is Wq 111 in Wotquenne's, whereas the concerto listed as Wq 1 turns up as H 403 (because Bach wrote *a lot* of music for solo keyboard). Actually, that H 1 isn't quite correct. It's actually H 1.5, because there are four earlier pieces, two marches and two polonaises, which were formerly attributed to J. S. Bach but which are now actually thought to have been written by C. P. E. Helm accounts for this gray area by numbering them 1/1–4, and hedges his bets a bit by calling that minuet number 1.5.

There is one more recent and particularly fascinating story involving the recovery and cataloguing of C. P. E.'s music. After the death of his daughter Anna Carolina Philippina in 1804, the last remains of Bach's estate were auctioned off. This material included most of his still-existing manuscripts along with music by other members of the Bach family, some dating back over a century and copied by J. S. Bach himself. The ultimate purchaser of a good portion of this legacy turned out to be Abraham Mendelssohn, father of composer Felix Mendelssohn, and one of a number of wealthy Jewish Berlin families devoted to the music of the Bachs (more on this later; it gets really interesting). This music in turn was donated in 1811 to the Berlin Sing-Akademie, to which Mendelssohn and many in his family belonged and historically had supported.

During the Second World War, the Nazis packed up the Sing-Akademie library for safekeeping. This turned out to be futile. The Russians ransacked the castle where the collection was stored, and during their retreat dropped it off for some reason in Kiev. There it remained, in a museum basement, lost to the world until it was rediscovered largely intact in 1999. The collection, thousands of items strong, contained over five hundred articles directly relating to the Bach family and to C. P. E. in particular, including most of the vocal music which had long been thought lost. After a lengthy negotiation, the collection was repatriated to Germany in 2001, and music scholars have been having a field day ever since. This discovery, combined with the power of the internet and the prospect of a slew of unpublished material seeing the light of day for the first time as part of the new C. P. E. Bach Complete Works, has raised his profile in a hitherto undreamt of way. He has become, two hundred years after his death, a vibrant subject of conversation once again.

I am offering this information because, first, it highlights some very real musicological issues that it doesn't hurt to know about, and second, because it really is interesting to see how the situation with Bach's music has reached its present state. It is also useful to note that the ongoing complete edition just mentioned, published under the auspices of the Packard Humanities Institute and a bit over 50 percent complete at time of writing, is organized strictly by genre and source (that is, whether a work was previously published or remained in manuscript until now). It uses Wq numbers as primary identifiers and supplements these as necessary with H numbers, an eminently sensible solution that I have also adopted in the tables of works that I have prepared for this book.

Since Wotquenne and Helm, still more catalogs have been prepared (such as Kast's), but you really don't need to bother with these as long as you understand the organizing concept behind the two main ones. If you need to identify specific works, you will be fine if you know the Wq number or, failing that, the H number, and many recordings offer both. If I don't offer multiple identifiers in discussing the music on the following pages, it is only because I am keeping matters as simple as possible. If you wish to explore the catalogs at your leisure, you can find both Wotquenne and Helm very easily online, and there is even a concordance that allows you to navigate between them. The important thing, for our purposes, is that you should be able easily to identify and find whatever piece of music catches your fancy, and that I can guarantee.

Part 1

Getting Started

1 Introducing the Other *Bach*

A mere technician . . . can lay no claim to the rewards of those who sway in gentle undulation the ear rather than the eye, the heart rather than the ear, and lead it where they will.

—C. P. E. Bach[1]

Perhaps the most remarkable observations we can make in considering the career of Carl Philipp Emanuel Bach stem from comparing the outward dullness of his placid, dutiful, comfortably middle-class life to the volcanic, disruptive, passionate intensity of the music that he wrote. There is no clue in his biography that explains the depth and force of emotion that he so powerfully sought to express. This doesn't mean that Bach suffered no sorrows or that his career was an unwavering pageant of success; but judging by the standards of the day his path was comparatively straightforward, and free of the turmoil that we constantly encounter in listening to the music itself. We can't explain it, and there's no point in trying. Contemporaneous composers in North Germany wrote in similar style, so there was definitely something "in the air," aesthetically speaking, but the sheer force of personality and originality that C. P. E. consistently displayed over the course of six decades of active composing remain an astounding achievement by any standard.

Few would argue with the proposition that a sequel is almost never as good as the original, whether in film, literature, or any other art. Moreover, when the original is Johann Sebastian Bach, a composer who has come as close to being deified as any cultural icon can be, then even to suggest that his offspring might be just as good, never mind better in certain areas, risks losing all credibility from the very start. Nevertheless, it is a fact that if you lived in North Germany in the latter half of the eighteenth century and enjoyed music by Bach, you would most likely have been thinking of Carl Philipp Emanuel, and not his father. He was "the great" Bach.

When a composer of arguable greatness like C. P. E. Bach suffers a couple of centuries of comparative neglect, the reasons are bound to be as interesting and complex as they are irrelevant to our modern-day enjoyment. In this introduction I hope to accomplish three objectives: first, to set the stage for listening by looking at Bach's life and career—a relatively simple task since, although his life was long and productive, his biography is quite short. Next, we'll look as some of the historical justifications for his neglect. These arguments, as you will see, essentially boil down to very subjective questions of aesthetics, which is just a fancy way of saying "taste." Finally, we will explore the more practical and, for that reason, valid reasons for C. P. E. Bach's relative absence from the repertoire.

A "Little" Biography, Really

Carl Philipp Emanuel was born on March 8, 1714. He was J. S. Bach's fifth child and his second surviving son, behind Wilhelm Friedemann, who also became a composer. J. S. famously had twenty children, but only ten survived to adulthood. The mother of this first batch of Bachs, Maria Barbara, died in 1720. The year of C. P. E.'s birth, 1714, is an important one in musical history. The great operatic reformer Christoph Willibald Gluck was born in the same year (dying a scant year before C. P. E.). When Bach senior died in 1750, his second son was already thirty-six years old and musically very well established—for over a decade—as keyboard accompanist to Frederick the Great, the flute-playing king of Prussia. The story of J. S. Bach's appearing at court in 1747 and improvising a fugue on a theme provided by Frederick, later working it up into a suite of works under the title "The Musical Offering," remains a seminal moment in Bach family history.

What this means practically is not just that C. P. E. grew up under the watchful eye and enjoyed the incomparable tutelage of his genius father, but that the father had plenty of time to avail himself of the latest developments being promulgated by his genius son. Of course, we will never know exactly how the two worked together and to what degree they may have influenced each other—we will return to this theme later in considering the keyboard concertos—but that there was mutual give and take between them, there can be no doubt. In any case, J. S. never sounds very much like C. P. E., and more significantly for our purposes, C. P. E. never comes across as a pale imitation of J. S.

This is a remarkable testimony to the younger Bach's strength of character. One only need consider how, for example, Richard Wagner's hapless son Siegfried tried desperately, and failed miserably, to escape the stifling legacy of his own father; and Siegfried had a big advantage over C. P. E. Bach in that Richard Wagner died when his son was still in his early teens. J. S. Bach, on the other hand, not only trained several highly gifted, musical children, but he made sure that they were *independently* musical, both from him and from each other. That was quite an achievement, and a tribute to his methods. When, in an autobiographical sketch written in 1773 and lasting a whopping half-dozen pages, C. P. E. claimed that he had had no other teacher than his father, he said it with pride, knowing that his musical pedigree was second to none.

Musical training aside, the broad outlines of C. P. E. Bach's life couldn't be simpler. His father was anxious that his sons have the advantage of a university education and the option of a career outside the field of music. Carl Philipp accordingly read law in Leipzig, and after 1733 at Frankfurt-Oder, all the while making money on the side as a keyboard player and occasional composer. In 1738 he was asked to join the retinue of then Prince Frederick II of Prussia, gaining a formal appointment on Frederick's accession to the throne in 1740. Bach remained in Berlin for the next twenty-eight years, before taking over from his godfather Georg Philipp Telemann as director of music for the Hamburg churches, in which position he stayed until his death in 1788 at the age of seventy-four.

That's it, basically. C. P. E. Bach never traveled widely, although he admittedly missed the opportunity and thought it would have been good for his reputation. He married happily in 1744 and had three children, two sons and a daughter. His elder son became a lawyer, while the younger was a talented painter who died in 1778, at about thirty years of age. Bach's wife and daughter survived him for some time, while the older son passed away the year following his own death. In the nineteenth century Bach acquired the reputation as a cheapskate because (a) his stepmother Anna Magdalena Bach died in poverty, and (b) he reportedly had the publisher's plates for the first edition of his father's swansong, *The Art of Fugue*, melted down and sold for scrap. That they were no longer needed seems not to have mattered to a posterity enthusiastically devoted to the process of placing J. S. Bach on the pedestal from which he still gazes down on the rest of us mere mortals.

Against this accusation must be accounted C. P. E. Bach's support and training of his brother, Johann Christian "the London" Bach; his decades of financial assistance to his sister; his care for his younger son during his lengthy final illness; and in general the fact that he left his family in excellent economic shape at the time of his death—a most unusual achievement. C. P. E. was in fact a very astute businessman, and one of the first composers to make a good living publishing and selling his own music. Although technically a municipal employee of the City of Hamburg for the last two decades of his life, he ran a highly successful and complex sales operation out of his home with the participation of his wife and daughter. Almost all of his surviving letters consist of transactional correspondence with his publisher, and the Big Topic of discussion in most of them is the high cost of postage, how to avoid paying it, and the hideously complex issue of currency conversion between the various German and foreign states and principalities. This doesn't mean that he was cheap—frugal rather, and cautious.

C. P. E. took great pride in his education, and cultivated friendships with noted scholars, poets, writers, and other representatives of the German educated classes. He also amassed an impressive collection of musicians' portraits, some four hundred in all, which was dispersed after his death. Happily, thanks to the Estate Catalog mentioned in the Preface, we know what was in the collection, and for the ongoing

Complete Works published by the Packard Humanities Institute its contents have been reassembled and printed in two inexpensive and fascinating volumes. In short, we know enough about C. P. E.'s life to know just how unfortunate it is that we know so little. As time goes on and more information trickles in, thanks to the latest scholarship, it becomes increasingly clear just how true this assumption must be.

For the most part, though, if you read any of the current C. P. E. Bach biographies, you will be struck by the fact that the first few chapters generally start with a statement along the lines of, "Very little is known about Bach's time at . . . ," or "The circumstances remain obscure concerning his relationship with . . . ," and so forth. This is usually followed by an extensive discussion of what we theoretically ought to know but don't, because while the details of C. P. E.'s life from moment to moment are pretty much lost to us, we are privy to a great deal of information about his environment and the culture of the period in which he lived.

For example, musical life at the court of Frederick the Great (1712–86) has been studied extensively. Frederick was quite a character. His father, Frederick William I, was a despotic monster with some very strange ideas about child rearing. The fact that his son quite likely was gay probably didn't help. When Frederick II attempted to flee to England in 1730 with his companion Hans Hermann von Katte, a lieutenant in the Prussian army, both were arrested and imprisoned, and Frederick II was forced to watch Katte's subsequent decapitation. After his characteristically arranged marriage in 1733, an event which prompted the prince to consider suicide, Frederick II settled for having nothing whatsoever to do with his wife. It certainly was not unusual for married couples to sleep in separate bedrooms in those days; the prince and his wife slept in separate palaces.

Frederick I had no time for the *musical* arts generally; he insisted that his son learn useful things, such as the art of war, and in fact once he was released from prison Frederick II turned out to be just as interested in that as he was in playing the flute. He was actually a military genius. He annexed a couple of provinces at the first opportunity and beat just about everyone during the Seven Years' War (1756–63).

Under him Prussia became a world power, but all of this would come somewhat later.

Frederick II finally ascended the throne in 1740, and proceeded to earn his moniker "the Great." He presided over a cultural and intellectual flowering of truly impressive magnitude. Voltaire was his buddy. After flute playing, Frederick's major musical passion was opera. He wrote several of his own librettos and insisted, among other things, that composers tailor their works to his precise specifications, and that the singers sing them exactly as written (an unheard-of practice at the time). Ever the perfectionist, he was always on hand, looking over the shoulder of his conductor during the performances to catch any mistakes or deviations and correct the musicians on the spot. Unsurprisingly, and given his relatively unadventurous musical tastes, no operas produced under Frederick's watchful eye and ear have made it into the modern repertoire (although some have been revived and recorded).

Among the musicians that Frederick gathered around him was flute virtuoso Johann Joachim Quantz, and between them they composed nearly three hundred flute sonatas for Frederick's personal use. The king himself wrote 121 of them, while Quantz additionally churned out several hundred flute concertos. Frederick was, to use the oxymoronic term, every inch an "enlightened despot." He banned torture, for example, although depending on how you feel about listening to three hundred flute sonatas, you might say that he merely replaced it with more creative measures.

Adding luster to the king's cultural program, Quantz published an extremely influential treatise on flute playing, a work which, together with Johann Agricola's manual on singing and C. P. E. Bach's *Essay on the True Art of Keyboard Playing* (1753) established the Berlin court as the center of European musical pedagogy. These works offer valuable information on eighteenth-century performance practice, and they are still widely used by today's historically informed performance movement. Bach's treatise in particular became an instant classic, and it remains so for its clarity, practicality, and comprehensiveness. When his reputation as a composer was at its lowest, the *Essay* ("*Versuch*" in German) served to keep C. P. E.'s name alive as an important figure in the history of eighteenth-century music. It also sold well, its two parts running through several editions in Bach's lifetime.

If Frederick valued C. P. E. as an accompanist, he seems to have had little time for him as a composer. Given the way that posterity has treated the names that the king did value, this may have been a blessing. Freed of the obligation to accommodate the royal taste, Bach rapidly developed a personal style that was appreciated by musical Berlin, and embodied in a substantial production of works of all kinds. Still, thirty years of accompanying flute sonatas and furnishing the keyboard parts in boring operas has to wear on one's patience, and the pay was nothing to shout about either—at least in Bach's view. By 1767, when the opportunity came to make the move to Hamburg, he was more than ready.

In fact, Bach had been ready for years. Twice in the 1750s he had tried to take over his father's job as director of music for the Leipzig churches, but was rejected each time. Hamburg offered C. P. E. the chance to live and work with a freedom that he had never before known. A free city which had been part of the mercantile Hanseatic League since the Middle Ages, the penurious city fathers balked at spending serious money on church music. They were content to have Bach make arrangements of older works, including those by the recently deceased Telemann, sacred music composer Gottfried Homilius, and even his own father. This got him through both the regular holidays and the special occasions that came up from time to time. Originality was never a priority, and quality could be taken for granted. If the actual performance level was indifferent at best, no one felt much inclined to complain. Bach's characteristic level of industry and organizational acumen took care of the rest.

So, with the church music situation under control, Bach was free to pursue an independent career as a freelance composer. There were times when he could combine both his day job and his other activities, as when he composed his three sacred oratorios for performance in either church or concert hall, and at the public concerts that Bach organized, he often included a healthy sprinkling of sacred choral music (Handel being a particular favorite); but the only limiting factors on his activities were time and the willingness of the public to pay for whatever he had to offer. It was, in most respects, an ideal situation for a man of his talents and entrepreneurial zeal, and he made the most of it.

History Without Pity

So, as you can plainly see, with the information we have about his time composing for Berlin and Hamburg we can talk about C. P. E.'s situation and work environment endlessly, but what we still can't do is speak in much detail about the man himself. As a subject for scholarship in music Bach represents relatively new terrain. It is impossible to become well acquainted with his output without coming to the conclusion that few composers have gotten such a bad deal from the vagaries of history, and modern academics have only just begun to redress the injustice done to his genius and reputation. Art history in general, and music history particularly, often can be described as "winner's history," written in hindsight so as to emphasize the direct line of descent of those select qualities that later generations deem important or worthy of imitation or emulation. It is too often narrowly focused, subjective, and pitiless.

C. P. E. stood on the wrong side of history in a double sense, first by the mere fact of his being his father's son, and second because he was not a member of the First Viennese School of Haydn, Mozart, and Beethoven. This was the group that set the standards of form and style for virtually all types of instrumental music that came later. The view of C. P. E. as second rate, and the resultant labeling of him as merely "historically interesting," was both ill considered and inaccurate. The arbitrary shape of the standard paradigm of musical development in the eighteenth century can be shown quite easily by noting the fact that the evolutionary line—as currently taught—allegedly passes right through the German high baroque that culminated in J. S. Bach and Handel, and from there leads directly on to the First Viennese School. Meanwhile Bach's immediate successors, including his pupils and his own children, are sidelined almost entirely. If we were talking about geometry, this is like saying that the shortest distance between two points involves taking a sharp, ninety-degree turn midway between them.

There is no question that C. P. E.'s music is less *important* in terms of what came later than is the music of the First Viennese School, but historical importance should not be confused with aesthetic viability and artistic value. Music is especially difficult to judge in this respect because of the time factor. To be assessed properly it has to be played, and played well, persistently, over time. Works that may have been extremely popular or influential in their day, as C. P. E. Bach's undoubtedly were, but which did not remain so over time, may well come to be viewed as historically marginal. But this does not mean that they are bad music. In his lifetime C. P. E. was one of the most widely admired composers in Europe, and his admirers included Haydn, Mozart, and Beethoven.

However, even this last fact can be, and was, viewed in a way that shines an unfavorable light onto the actual music. The argument goes something like this: Because the great Viennese composers admired C. P. E., they took a few of the most "relevant" and "valid" elements of his style, jettisoned the rest, and improved them beyond all recognition in perfecting their own musical language. Bach's work thus becomes a sort of junkyard to be exploited and salvaged by later and greater names, while the basic obsolescence of his own music is reaffirmed. Of course, artists borrow stylistic traits and ideas from one another all the time, and the borrowers may use them in ways undreamt of by the lenders; but again, the act of borrowing need not diminish the worth of the original source. Bach, as I have no doubt you will agree, achieved a level of perfection in his own style that nothing subsequently could devalue. A Bach sonata is not a Mozart sonata, but both are affective and entertaining vehicles for emotional expression, with the choice between them simply being a matter of personal preference.

C. P. E. Bach's life covered a period of astounding change in musical aesthetics—changes for which he was at least partly responsible. When he was born in 1714, Vivaldi was hard at work perfecting the baroque violin concerto, and the three-movement structure still in use today was a new invention. When Bach died in 1788, Mozart had already written *Don Giovanni*, a work with elements that foreshadow the later, romantic period. C. P. E.'s own music encompasses all of this, and it is his faithfulness to certain elements of baroque style, combined with his hugely expanded range of contrasts and sentiment, that proved so disconcerting to nineteenth-century scholars and performers. In short, his music was very difficult to categorize, partly because that of his North German colleagues was even less well known—and so the necessary context to understand his achievement was lacking—and partly because he was, truly, a very original musical voice that fits tidily into no single category. This heterogeneity has led some writers to label C. P. E. Bach's style as "immature."

To give some color to these claims, and help us understand the impact they had in creating a dismissive historical perception of C. P. E.'s music, I have prepared a timeline that contrasts his creative life with significant musical milestones in the wider European world. Many of these contemporaneous "major moments," by definition, follow the conventional path staked out in the standard view of Western musical history. That is, they chart the theoretical march of "progress" from the late baroque idiom of Bach, Handel, Rameau, and their contemporaries, through the alleged wasteland of the galant and rococo styles in the 1760s and '70s, and culminating in the glorious emergence of the Viennese classics.

Don't get me wrong: those Viennese classics are absolutely magnificent and their emergence was undoubtedly a signal moment in musical history. Nothing we conclude here can or should change that fact. The question we have to consider is whether or not our perception of this triumphant moment requires the denigration and dismissal of much that preceded or competed with it. Or to phrase the issue a bit differently: Is our conventional view of "the classics" threatened by the possibility that there may be other, possibly equally great music that has been overlooked, misjudged, or misunderstood?

The first problem that needs addressing is that of the so-called galant or rococo period. It's a difficult notion to pin down, describing a kind of music that was light, gracious, courtly, simple in texture, and sentimental. Much of it appeared between the 1750s and '80s, which is exactly contemporary with the late baroque and early classical periods. In North Germany it was not so much an era as a specific aesthetic movement, one that also encompassed the *empfindsamer Stil*, or "sensitive style," devoted to evoking rich shades of emotional expression. Musicologically speaking, this non-epoch is often viewed as a transitional moment, with all that this suggests for an art that is unripe or uncertain in its intent, neither one thing nor the other, and noteworthy only to the extent that it strives to be something new but never quite gets there. One of the principal exponents of the galant style was C. P. E. Bach's younger brother, Johann Christian (1735–82).

J. C. was only fourteen when his father died, and so he spent his later, musically formative years under the watchful eye of his older brother. C. P. E. disliked the younger Bach's simpler compositional style. Significantly J. C. became, for a time at least, a successful opera composer, whereas C. P. E. wrote none and had a certain disdain for the medium, comic opera in particular. The relationship between the two brothers was further strained by J. C.'s conversion to Catholicism. Fortified by time spent in Italy (a pedigree always viewed with suspicion in North German musical circles), J. C.'s generally short, sunny, melodic instrumental pieces became something of a watchword historically for musical shallowness. His music's charm, however, was not lost on the young Mozart, who met J. C. during his youthful sojourn in London, and arranged some of his solo sonatas as keyboard concertos.

So, on the one hand, J. C. gets a certain amount of credit for inspiring Mozart, but on the other hand Mozart's later music cast J. C.'s into oblivion until very recently, when (on recordings, at least) it has made something of a comeback. Proper consideration of J. C. Bach nonetheless must wait until a revival of his operas, since this was the field in which he wrote many of his most important pieces. In any case, the traditional charges leveled against the works of this era, that they lack both the contrapuntal interest of the baroque period as well as the tonal drama of the classical period, certainly do not hold much water with respect to C. P. E. Bach.

This isn't so much because such observations are not true, as much as it is because they ignore the possibility of great music being written along different lines entirely. For his contemporaries, C. P. E.'s music was all but unclassifiable. Christian Friedrich Daniel Schubart, in his *Aesthetics of Music* (1806) wrote admiringly of its individuality: "What one so often criticizes in his works is their stubborn attitude, frequent bizarre elements, intentional difficulty, complicated notation . . . and an uncompromising refusal to conform to fashionable taste." These qualities can be seen as both positive and negative, depending on your perspective, but they are hardly constituents of the rococo or galant styles, for all of the occasional similarities or the music's frequently evident desire to please.

The Practicalities of Performance

The vagaries of history, however, only comprise one factor out of an entire complex of reasons that explains C. P. E. Bach's neglect. There are serious musical and practical issues as well, and they can best be summed up by looking briefly at two very real problems concerning performance practice that must be addressed in performing him: ornamentation, and the basso continuo or "thorough bass." The question of ornamentation is the easier of the two to explain and understand. It involves the expectation that performers should decorate the music's basic text by adding trills, turns, melodic filigree, and assorted other doodads. It was a major feature of baroque performance, and it comprises much of the subject matter of Bach's famous *Essay*. Indeed, it is probably fair to say that Bach's treatise offered the most complete and clearly explained discussion of the topic published up to that time.

The purpose of ornamentation, in theory, is to enhance the melodic line by changing its sound and shape. Trills can make happy music even giddier; appoggiaturas (dissonant "leaning" tones that demand resolution) help to convey sadness or melancholy; turns of various kinds add grace and elegance; vibrato enhances vocal expressivity and timbral warmth. Embellishments, Bach insisted, "connect and enliven tones and impart stress and accent; they make music pleasing and awaken our close attention. Expression is heightened by them; let a piece be sad, joyful, or otherwise, and they will lend a fitting assistance." Without ornaments, Bach continues, "the best melody is empty and ineffective, the clearest content clouded."[2]

Properly applied, the use of ornaments also draws attention to the taste and virtuosity of the performer, hopefully in a way that never diminishes the emotional impact of the work. Needless to say, the invitation to embellish lends itself to abuse by overzealous or narcissistic singers and players, and faced with this very common problem a composer has two choices. Gluck chose the first path, namely, to eliminate as much ornamentation as he dared and get back to the basics of simple, expressive melody. His "reform" operas embody this principle and set the standard for the medium in the classical era and beyond. Bach chose a different, less drastic, but no less legitimate route: leave as little to chance as possible by notating much of the intended ornamentation, and give plenty of useful guidance for the rest.

So, although Bach expected and encouraged his performers to embellish his melodic lines, if they couldn't, or didn't, the music still could be played exactly as written with fully satisfying results. Indeed, the necessity of additional ornamentation in Bach's music is something of a myth, one promulgated by the success of his *Essay* and his reputation as a theoretician. In modern times, at least until very recently, this has resulted in the belief among some players that his works require a degree of specialization that many have neither the time nor the inclination to acquire. The success of Bach as an icon of period practice overshadows the reality of Bach the practical composer, whose scores set an unusually high standard in their notational detail, precision, and clarity.

One of Bach's most popular publications was a series of keyboard sonatas and other pieces "with varied reprises." These go beyond the mechanics of mere decorative ornamentation to reveal how a truly creative composer/performer should engage with the work being played, offering examples of free variations on the principal melodic ideas. Theoretically these would be improvised on the spot, but in writing all of this down Bach tacitly acknowledged the fact that the art of spontaneous variation and improvisation was dying out. The newly emergent classical style heralded by Gluck stressed simplicity of means and (relative) fidelity to the composer's score. So, even if Bach's use of ornamentation and his systematic presentation of the topic in the *Essay* demonstrated its continuing viability as a compositional tool, his innovations, historically, could not withstand the challenge offered by music written in an entirely different style.

Fortunately the period instrument movement has spent the past several decades recovering the lost arts of ornamentation and improvisation.

With that has come a newfound respect for Bach's achievements in this area, and a far greater understanding of their degrees of applicability to performances of his music. Historically informed artists, never mind jazz musicians and whole schools of the musical avant-garde, have also demolished the common prejudice which asserts that leaving important elements up to the performer must be somehow more primitive or "missing something" that the most modern, very fully notated music enjoys. Still more pertinently, Bach's musical materials were startlingly new in their own day and they still sound remarkably fresh in ours. Using ornaments to help keep them that way is as valid and sensible a strategy now as it was then. It doesn't date.

After explaining the correct use of ornamentation, the issue that concerns Bach the most in his *Essay* is proper realization of the basso continuo, or "thorough bass" part. This device offers a sort of musical shorthand to accompanists, permitting them to fill in the music's bass line with the necessary supporting harmonies. It's really not that much different than a guitar chart showing the series of chords that permits a player to strum through a song, although continuo playing has a wider field of application. It appears in orchestral, choral, and chamber music, and especially in the type of operatic "sung speech" known as secco (dry) recitative, where the keyboard lightly underpins rapid vocal dialogue. How to read "figured bass" notation, as it's called—when to fill in the harmony and to what degree—comprises an art in itself. You may well ask at this point why the bass line needed to be elaborated in the first place, and the answer to this question reveals some important facts about the aesthetics of our musical culture.

At least until the twentieth century, when the avant-garde started challenging the very definition of music, it was taken for granted that the most perfect musical instrument was the human voice, and all mechanical devices designed to emit musical tones aspired to imitate it. Accordingly, musical instruments fell into two basic categories: melody instruments limited (more or less) to playing one note at a time, such as the flute or violin, and accompanying instruments, such as keyboards, harps, lutes, and other members of the guitar family. Their job was to provide the necessary harmonic support for the "singing" instruments that got the tunes. Instrumental music, texturally, consisted of these solo, vocal-style lines on top; a nice firm bass on the bottom; and harmonic "filler" in the middle provided by the accompanists and called the continuo, for the simple reason that harmonic continuity is what it supplied.

This remained the situation until the composers of the First Viennese School in the latter half of the eighteenth century figured out that instruments did not necessarily need this additional support. They could form ensembles in which each performer, or instrumental group, could function both in solo and supporting roles. The result was a true revolution: the birth of the modern orchestra, and the creation of chamber ensembles such as the string quartet, wind quintet, and others in various combinations. The invention of the pianoforte also permitted keyboard instruments to participate effectively in this new concept of instrumental sonority.

However, when it came to writing instrumental or ensemble music, Bach retained the system inherited from the baroque era of including figured bass parts for keyboard accompaniment. This was the other aspect of his style that was later regarded as obsolete, particularly as the art of playing from a figured bass line died out in the early nineteenth century, at the same time that the piano supplanted all of the other keyboard instruments that Bach had used (except the organ, which was and remains a special case). The situation with respect to actual performance doomed his works to oblivion as long as newly composed music remained popular; in other words, until a taste for "the classics" of a bygone era evolved to the point where artists and audiences welcomed exploration of earlier styles of performance.

Bach truly believed that "no piece can be well performed without some form of keyboard accompaniment. Even in heavily scored works, such as operas performed out of doors, where no one would think that the harpsichord could be heard, its absence can certainly be felt. And from a position above the performers all of its tones are clearly perceptible."[3] His conviction regarding the desirability of the continuo, then, was not some mindless adherence to an old tradition, but the practical result of his own experience as a performing musician based on a thoroughly considered view of how the music ought to sound.

Bach's use of the continuo was, accordingly, anything but routine. As with his thoughtfully embellished melodic lines, his care in notating figured bass parts was unprecedentedly precise, detailed, and above all, texturally aware. His orchestral scores indicate plainly when to fill in the harmonies, when to play the bass line only ("*tasto solo*"), when to use bare octaves in both hands, and even when the keyboard should remain silent. These possibilities always enhance the music's expressive meaning and provide contrasts of light and shade. In this respect his music is more "modern" than the contemporaneous works of the Viennese masters, at least to the extent that it eliminates possible ambiguities in performance.

In particular, it's generally understood that although much Viennese classical orchestral music technically does not require a keyboard accompaniment, a continuo part was often added anyway. The position of the conductor, in the modern sense, did not yet exist, and orchestras were led from the first violin or from the keyboard, which doubtless assisted in keeping everyone together. But what did the accompanist actually play, and when? We have almost no idea. You won't, for instance, find a single figured bass part in any early Haydn symphony, although performers routinely add them, and in doing so just as routinely destroy the music's scheme of contrasts by imposing undesired harmonies, distracting rhythmic patterns or accents, and creating textural monotony. Bach was aware of this practice and spoke out strongly against it.

Nonetheless, the very fact that he had to make a point of the desirability of the continuo in his music when writing the *Essay* suggests that its automatic presence was being questioned, at least in larger orchestras. It really depends on the piece. Bach's string symphonies, for instance, certainly require the continuo. Modern performances of his keyboard concertos however, especially on piano, sometimes avail themselves of the option of minimizing or leaving it out and still sound just fine. Taking this option highlights the contrasting character of the soloist and conforms to more current views of how the featured instrument should function in a concerto. Bach likely knew that he was bucking a trend in retaining his allegiance to continuo playing, but in expressing his preference he certainly wasn't being dogmatic about it.

Today, with the baroque revival an accomplished fact and the presence of the continuo in orchestral and chamber music no longer unusual or unfamiliar to classical music listeners, Bach's instrumental output suffers from none of the circumstances that hindered its acceptance historically. In this respect he has benefited from the trends that brought the music of his father and earlier masters back into the active repertoire, but there is also yet another way in which musicology has come to the rescue. We no longer see music history as a triumphant, evolutionary parade from lesser or more primitive forms and idioms to higher ones. It was this attitude that led to the sidelining of baroque music in the first place, including much of the output of J. S. Bach and Handel.

C. P. E. Bach has had to wait a very long time for his day to come, but what matters now is that it *has* come. The process began in musicological circles, and has finally made it out into the wider world. As early as 1960, Bach scholar and cataloguer E. Eugene Helm was able to claim:

> During recent years there has been a steadily increasing interest in the life and works of C. P. E. Bach (usually called Emanuel Bach during his lifetime), second son of J. S. Bach and probably the greatest of all Frederick [the Great's] musical servants. He has come out from under his father's shadow to be recognized as an original genius whose works not only supply many of the formal, technical, and aesthetic sources of classic and romantic music, but are in themselves great and provocative works of art.[4]

So, instead of dwelling further all of the reasons why C. P. E. Bach's music was not played and enjoyed for all of those lost years, it's time to open our ears and hear what special pleasures it has to offer.

2 Listening to C. P. E.

Since I have never loved excessive uniformity in composition and taste, have heard so much good work of such varied sorts, and have always been of the opinion that one should accept the good wherever it may be, even if to be found only in small measure in a piece; all this, along with my God-given natural talent, presumably accounts for the diversity of my compositions, which has often been noted.

—C. P. E. Bach, *Autobiography*[5]

A musician cannot move others unless he too is moved. He must of necessity feel all of the affects that he hopes to arouse in his audience, for the revealing of his own humor will stimulate a like humor in the listener. . . . Above all, he must discharge this office in a piece which is highly expressive by nature, whether it be by him or someone else.

—C. P. E. Bach, *Essay*[6]

It can be seen from the many affects which music portrays, that the accomplished musician must have special endowments and be capable of employing them wisely. He must carefully appraise the audience, their attitude toward the expressive content of his program, the place itself, and other additional factors. Nature has wisely provided music with every kind of appeal so that all might share in its enjoyment. It thus becomes the duty of the performer to satisfy to the best of his ability every last kind of listener.

—C. P. E. Bach, *Essay*[7]

In things that are to be printed, and therefore are for everyone, be less artistic and give more sugar.

—C. P. E. Bach, letter of 31 August 1784
to Johann Christoph Kühnau[8]

Because I was obliged to compose most of my works for certain persons and for the public, I have always been more restricted than in the few pieces composed only for myself. Occasionally I have even had to fulfill ridiculous specifications; yet for all that, it may be that such unpleasant circumstances have challenged my genius to certain inventions I might not otherwise have happened upon.

—C. P. E. Bach, *Autobiography*[9]

Listening to C. P. E. Bach's music offers an experience like no other. The better you get to know it, the more distinctive and original it sounds. Because he had the inclination and opportunity to write about his artistic aims extensively, both in the *Essay* as well as in occasional letters and the various prefaces to published editions of his works, there is very little ambiguity about his views as an artist. The above quotations provide a typical sample of his thinking about style, expression, and the relationship between the composer/performer and his audience. It is a remarkably generous, broad-minded vision: practical as well as idealistic, critical but not cynical, humble but honestly confident of mastery (and unafraid to say so). In this chapter, we will examine closely three of the keyboard pieces included for listening with this book in order to get acquainted with Bach's astonishingly personal idiom.

Solfeggio in C Minor, Wq 117/2 (1766)

In a posthumous career full of ironies, there is none greater than the fact that for some two centuries after his death Bach was represented in the public mind by this little piece, and none other. It was, and still is, a required challenge for virtually every piano student. Bach's total output for solo keyboard plays for approximately thirty-five hours and comprises several hundred individual pieces. The solfeggio lasts less than a minute. But even so this little piece contains quite a bit that is typical of its composer, however tiny the scale.

A solfeggio, technically, is a teaching piece for singers. This one sometimes also goes by the title "Solfeggietto," which just means "little solfeggio." Both names are based on the method of learning to sing at sight by sounding out the notes of the scale: do, re, mi, fa, sol, la, ti (si in Europe). In other words, as adapted for instrumental use, the piece is an etude, or study. Indeed, this particular example sounds very much like a lost bit of an etude by, perhaps, Chopin, and when I first heard it decades ago that is what I thought it was. There is an excellent chance that you already know it, too, perhaps without being able to say how or where you may first have heard it, and therein lies the first musical quality that we often encounter in C. P. E. Bach: it sounds like a more "modern" piece than it really is.

This quality of timelessness is very hard to pin down exactly; it's more a matter of subjective feeling than of objective fact, but it's quite real nonetheless. I'm not sure what 1766 sounded like, and I can't say what qualities you believe music of that period should have, but one thing I do know: you could make a plausible case for the solfeggio's having been written just about anytime during the late eighteenth or nineteenth century. Part of the reason for this no doubt stems from the music's perfect suitability to its purpose. It captures an aspect of keyboard technique that is universal and as valid today as it was in 1766.

In this particular case, at each of the principal theme's four appearances, the challenge Bach sets for the musician is to create a perfectly even flow of notes out of a single line of music divided between the two hands, while playing at the fastest possible tempo. This in turn suggests the second quality characteristic of so much of Bach's music: virtuosity.

Except for the very simplest pieces, none of Bach's music really is easy, even when he describes it as such, or designates a work for amateurs. A piece may be ingratiating from the listener's point of view, one of those moments when Bach decides to reward his audience with a bit of extra "sugar," but (much like his father) he seldom spares the player. Of course, any composer can write music that is technically difficult; the key is to write music that is both difficult and rewarding, to place the virtuosity in the service of art. As with Chopin's etudes, there is no more telling instance of this ability than when an alleged teaching piece also becomes equally, as here, a perfect little gem of musical expression.

This fact highlights another very important and noteworthy quality of C. P. E. Bach's music more generally: it is extremely expressive. The solfeggio flies by so quickly that you may not at first catch everything that goes on in it, but on repeated listening you will quickly realize that even here Bach has created a little dramatic scene. The minor key alone guarantees a certain level of inherent pathos, but what's so remarkable is that Bach takes very specific and easily audible steps to raise the level of tension at every moment that he can, and in a piece that lasts only fifty-three seconds, there can only be so many opportunities. In order to understand how he does it, we need to understand the solfeggio's form.

As previously mentioned, the main theme gets played four times. In between these appearances Bach inserts episodes based on different material. So, we have seven tiny sections in all: four statements of the theme, and three episodes. What is more, the third episode is a variation of the second. The form, then, looks like this: ABACAC'A. Lasting only about six seconds, the main theme contains two phrases, each of which has the same shape, forming a steadily rising sequence. This, combined with the evenness of the rhythm and the rapid tempo, produces a feeling of anxious striving.

The first episode maintains the same steadiness of rhythm and rapid-fire interplay of the two hands (in a good performance you should hear a perfect smoothness of the musical line). However, notice that the direction of the melodic pattern now descends. This means that after another six seconds, when the main theme returns in a different minor key, it is now in a lower part of the keyboard than at the start. This gives it a slightly darker timbre, and we start to feel that the tune has shifted to a different place. In other words, the opening theme is the traveler on this particular musical journey.

Things get even more interesting in the second episode. This has its own teeny, tiny form: CDCD, and it begins to disrupt the steady rhythm that the music has enjoyed to this point. Now the hands separate and while the right keeps up the basic pace, the left pounds out two stern, descending long tones, alternating with a nervous but static pulsation. Again, the general direction of these gestures is down, and so when the main theme returns for the third time, it appears at the lowest and darkest pitch yet. This gesture brings about a crisis, as the third episode begins with long notes in the left hand that stop the music dead in its tracks.

The sudden halt to what has hitherto been uninterrupted motion comes as a shock, and Bach heightens the intensity in every way possible. The dynamics shift from piano to forte as the left hand descends, the length of the actual descent now encompasses three notes in one long sequence instead of just two notes alternating with a different texture, and the right hand tries to restart its steady rhythm but pulls up short twice, as if confused as to where it is and how to get back on track. With a third effort, however, the music does manage to find its rhythm, returning to that nervous pulsation first heard in the second episode, and leading inexorably back to the main theme in its original position and so on to the end, closing with the melody at its highest point.

This little piece tells a story. A tune that wants to move upward finds itself caught in a process that causes it actually to move lower and lower on each repetition. This pattern could continue forever. It requires a dramatic rupture to stop it, and bring about an ultimate restoration of order. Two very prominent aspects of Bach's art are on display here. First, there is his love of surprise and drama expressed in strictly musical terms. Second, just consider the amount of variety that he packs into fifty-three seconds of music. There are seven distinct episodes containing contrasts in tonality, dynamics, texture, timbre, and rhythm. Above it all there is an exceptionally high level of craftsmanship. The composer's consideration for both the player and the listener produces music that is challenging, fun to play, and a pleasure to hear.

"L'Aly Rupalich" (La Bach), Wq 117/27 (1755)

Bach was, as mentioned previously, a great collector of portraits, and he even composed a few. Small, descriptive musical works such as this are known as character pieces, and during the baroque period they were a French specialty. The collections by such composers as Couperin and Rameau are the best known out of a huge and very attractive repertoire of harpsichord and chamber music. During the 1750s Bach developed an interest in the genre, and wrote some twenty-five musical portraits, not counting the ones that exist in multiple versions. "L'Aly Rupalich" has been described as a sketch of a trickster or joker, but its original title was "La Bach," and so there is some cause to believe that it refers to Bach himself, or perhaps one of his family. For this and a few other reasons it has intrigued scholars ever since its provenance first became known.

The piece is actually a dance called, for some reason, a murky. This isn't so much a form or style as it is a texture: a simple tune over a bouncing accompaniment in broken octaves. "Broken" just means that the notes are played sequentially rather than simultaneously, as with chords. This is what makes them bounce. Bach didn't think much of the murky, or more specifically its "drum bass." As you will see in the chapter on the keyboard music, Bach had disparaging things to say about this kind of accompaniment, but he nonetheless wrote a few pieces in the style. Perhaps because he regarded it as a comparatively silly and primitive effect, he deliberately played up these very qualities in "L'Aly Rupalich" to the point of grotesqueness, and the result is absolutely hilarious. Paul Corneilson, C. P. E. Bach scholar and managing editor of the Complete Works, describes the music as a "disco piece," and that's really how it sounds.

As an avowed practitioner of the "sensitive style," Bach has a reputation—well deserved, I might add—for writing music of flamboyant emotionality, and this usually means sadness, anger, and pathos. For reasons I leave to specialists in cultural psychoanalysis, happiness and humor don't often qualify as serious feelings, especially in the world of "art music." However, Bach was just as adept at depicting cheer as he was misery; indeed, it is his emotional *range* that is so extraordinary, the distance between the highs and the lows and the intensity of each—not just his expertise in expressing the darker side of life.

The truth is that sadness in music is much easier to depict than happiness because all you need to do, basically, is find a minor key, write a good tune, and stick with it. The effect is cumulative and arises from dwelling on the same mood over a relatively long stretch of time. Happiness, on the other hand, if not to sound merely bland, requires a much greater variety of tone and texture. This is why so much sad music is slow and cheerier music is quick. Capturing actual humor demands, in addition, a very precise sense of musical timing. A composer either has this quality or he does not. Like a sense of humor generally, it can't be learned or taught. Haydn was our musical tradition's greatest comic voice, but C. P. E. Bach had the gift, too, and he used it lavishly.

And now I have a request to make: Stop reading and if you haven't already done it, just listen to the music, preferably a few times. It's only two minutes and forty seconds long. You don't want me to spoil the fun by talking about the formal mechanics and, in effect, giving away all of the punch lines. We will get there shortly because the music does contain important stylistic fingerprints that I want to point out, but the humor really should speak for itself. Besides, nothing kills a joke more effectively than trying to explain why it's funny. So enjoy.

Hopefully having now heard the music and found it amusing, or at least peculiar, we can take a closer look. As an initial observation, and similar to the solfeggio, it's probably safe to say once again that this music really doesn't sound like something typical of 1755. Consider that Mozart wouldn't even be born until the following year, Haydn had yet to write his first symphony, and Beethoven was still a couple of decades in the future. Where on earth did this stuff come from? If "L'Aly Rupalich" isn't exactly disco, it's certainly closer to that than to anything else, and wholly original—a delightfully anomalous and disorienting couple of minutes.

Its form, though, is quite similar to that of the solfeggio, a very common type that goes by the formal name of rondo. In a rondo a recurring main theme, or ritornello, returns repeatedly, separated by episodes containing different material. That's all there is to it. C. P. E. Bach put his own special spin on this form, and we'll consider the "Bach brand" more closely in discussing the keyboard works that he actually designated as rondos. For now, suffice it to say that there is no limit on the number of episodes you can employ and a great deal of the fun in a rondo, at least in a humorous one like this, lies in how cleverly the composer handles the return of the ritornello. "L'Aly Rupalich," then, has a form that looks more or less as follows: ABA—C[A]AD[A]—[A]AEA.

The above outline incorporates a couple of special features. The dashes between sections indicate pauses. The creative use of silence is one of the hallmarks of C. P. E. Bach's style, and few composers found more clever and surprising places to insert a pause. The "A" represents the ritornello, while the versions of it in brackets [A] represent "fake-outs," where Bach wants us to think that the ritornello is back as a structural landmark, but it really is not. Toward the end, he even tricks us with a double fake-out: two different versions of the ritornello, or portions of it. Although separated by a sudden pause, neither signals a formal return to the original theme. How do we know this? Well, the first is missing its opening bar and seems to get diverted into a new episode before breaking off sharply. The second starts softly, in a sinister minor key, before the real ritornello bursts in boldly.

The ritornello theme itself has two important features. First, it consists of several short motives of differing lengths, separated by brief pauses. This is very typical of Bach's mature style in quick movements. These catchy, distinct fragments offer prime material for further development. The initial motive consists of just two descending notes, but it's so harmonically distinctive that every time you hear it you expect the ritornello to return, whether it does or not. This gives Bach license to tease us, beginning most of the episodes with the same two-note gesture. The second phrase (in "disco" rhythm) is immediately followed by a softly echoed, inexact repetition—again, a very common feature of Bach's thematic workmanship. His fondness for abrupt, quiet digressions breaks up the regularity of the phrases and adds an additional element of unpredictability. It is particularly affecting in minor keys.

Sudden shifts in dynamics and unpredictable accents feature in just about everything that Bach wrote. Composers before Bach's day tended to indicate dynamics simply by saying "loud" or "soft," and they seldom if ever changed volume in midtheme as his does constantly. Intermediate nuances, such as *mezzo piano* or *mezzo forte*, very soft and very loud (*pianissimo* and *fortissimo*), crescendos, decrescendos, and many details of accentuation were left to the discretion of the performers. Even with the dynamically challenged harpsichord, which must have been used for his music as often as not, Bach took exceptional care to notate volume levels fully, and his music demands careful attention to his indications. As late as the 1740s such composers as the Italian violinist and pedagogue Francesco Geminiani were still classifying dynamic nuances as "ornaments," but in this music there is nothing ornamental or optional about them. They are an integral part of the sonic fabric and thus the expressive message.

Bach constructs rondo episodes of every conceivable length. In "L'Aly Rupalich," Episode B is quite short, whereas C and D are considerably longer. Most interesting is Episode E. This is a coda whose harmonies clearly tell us that the end is coming—you can hear it just over the musical horizon—only it's not quite the end. The composer toys with our expectations once again and brings back the ritornello, but cuts it off in midphrase. The actual ending couldn't be more surprising (or funny). All of these techniques work equally well in Bach's more serious music; it's merely a question of emphasis and proportion, of knowing how and when to use your tools for maximum effect. A relatively dry description such as this, as I hope you have heard for yourself, can't really give a good sense of what a piece of music sounds like. I can describe the ingredients, but they only hint at the unique flavor of the finished dish.

Sonata in C Minor, Wq 50 No. 6 (1759)

This extraordinary sonata is the last in a series of six that Bach published as a set of "Sonatas with Varied Reprises." His stated his purpose in an absolutely marvelous preface to the printed edition:

Nowadays one cannot do without ornamentation of repeats. It is expected of every performer. One of my friends exerts all possible effort to perform a composition as it was written, cleanly and according to all rules of good execution; why should he not be applauded? Another has to rely on his prowess at ornamentation to hide his inability to express adequately the prescribed notes; and yet, the public prefers him to the first. Audiences want almost every idea ornamented on repetition, without always examining whether such procedure will suit the nature of the piece or the ability of the performer. Often, only this kind of ornamentation, especially when accompanied by a long and elaborately ornamented cadenza, will squeeze applause from most listeners. What misuse, therefore, of these two real virtues of performance! No one has the patience anymore to play the prescribed notes the first time through; the long absence of applause becomes unbearable. Often this premature ornamentation is against the sense of the composition, against the intended emotion, and against the way ideas should interrelate, a disagreeable thing to do to a composer. Assuming, however, that the performer possesses all the requisites to perform ornamentation properly, is he always in the mood for it? Might he not face new difficulties when tackling unknown repertoire? Isn't the principal aim of ornamentation to do honor to the performer as well as the composition? Shouldn't the repeat produce ideas as good as the original? Nevertheless, in spite of these difficulties and misuses, good ornamentation is always worthwhile. By the way, I am referring to what I said on the subject at the end of the first part of my *Essay*.

In writing these sonatas, I had mostly in mind beginners and amateurs who, on account of a certain age or other problems, have neither the patience nor enough time to practice sufficiently. I wanted to create for them the comfortable and easy pleasure of making themselves heard with ornamentations without having either to invent them for themselves or to have them dictated by others and to memorize them with great difficulty. Finally, I have clearly indicated what is essential for good performance, so these pieces can be played with freedom, even if one is not quite in the mood for it.

I am joyful to be, as far as I know, the first to have worked thus for the benefit and pleasure of my patrons and friends. How happy

> I should be if the special vigor of my pleasure to serve should be recognized in these efforts.
>
> Berlin, in the month of July 1759
>
> C. P. E. Bach[10]

In other words, what Bach has created is a sort of musical paint-by-numbers kit, a do-it-yourself guide to correct performance. He takes pains to stress the desirability of good ornamentation (and plug his *Essay* in the process), but what is really interesting is his suggestion that it can be just as desirable to use none at all. We need to distinguish between what performers tended to do, allegedly in response to audience demand, and what they should do. Bach makes it quite clear that he admires an interpretation that sticks strictly to the notes on the page if this best does justice to the work, and as I mentioned in the introduction, Bach's own music seldom *requires* extra help in the form of improvised ornamentation. As he writes in the *Essay*, "Above all things, a prodigal use of embellishments must be avoided. Regard them as spices which may ruin the best dish or gewgaws which may deface the most perfect building."[11] These sonatas illustrate this rule, and they are also important for what they tell us about the difference between *variation* and *ornamentation*.

The idea of variation lies at the heart of Bach's compositional method. He was an inveterate tinkerer, constantly revising, adjusting, and "renovating" (*erneuern*) earlier works. Probably he never played anything the same way twice, and his approach takes some getting used to because it's really unlike that of any other composer. There are many different types of variation in music, but as applied to a melody the concept is often thought of, inaccurately, as starting with the tune in its simplest form, and then making it progressively more elaborate by adding lots of ornaments while breaking the theme up into smaller and smaller note values. An excellent example of this type would be Handel's justly famous set of keyboard variations, "The Harmonious Blacksmith."

Bach does operate this way occasionally, particularly in the pieces that he designates as true "variations," and even to a certain extent in this very sonata. Most of the time, however, the initial theme is already so precisely notated that the process of variation does not so much consist of adding ornamental embellishments as it does swapping out whole bits of melody for something entirely new. The line between *variation* and *composition* gets a bit blurry in these instances, with the approach perhaps closer to a kind of jazz improvisation than anything else. Bach's own term, *erneuern*, usually gets translated as "revise," but it literally means "renew," and I prefer "renovate" because the result is often closer to a "gut rehab" in the construction industry, where you preserve a building's exterior structure but demolish and replace all of the interior details. This is clearly what Bach means when he asks, "Shouldn't the repeat produce ideas as good as the original?"

You may well be wondering at this point how the performer substitutes new ideas while remaining respectful of the composer's intent, never mind the expressive point of the work being played. Certainly it's not easy, and Bach was right to be concerned at what could happen to his music in the hands of musicians less accomplished than he was. Part of the answer to this conundrum lies in the fact that, for Bach, "the tune" was not the primary defining characteristic of the piece; the harmony was more important, because harmony determines the fundamental expressive impact of a theme or larger passage. In his music, melody arises naturally as the surface manifestation of the scheme of harmonies defined by the bass line. There is practically no limit to the number of individual but related themes, or "families" of themes, that he can create through this technique.

This means that Bach's ideas often have no single definitive shape; they exist as a series of variants the details of which can sound quite different from one another. Contemporary audiences noticed this aspect of his music immediately, and some found it disconcerting. For the listener unaccustomed to the approach and unwilling to give the music the time that it requires to become familiar, Bachian melodies can be difficult to grasp. They tend to avoid the kinds of internal symmetries and phrase repetitions that help a musical idea "stick." Each theme may be very beautiful or expressively striking—indeed, most of them are—but they don't fall into the sort of "greatest hits" category that you find in those old record collections of "one hundred immortal melodies" and the like. Think of listening to Bach's tunes as an experience akin to viewing the surface of a river. If you look closely, you will see numerous waves, ripples, and eddies, and no two are exactly alike; but however varied the surface, the main current always moves strongly in a single direction and the course of the river is carved in bedrock.

Bach was not out to confound his listeners. Just the opposite. He was concerned that his music sound perpetually fresh, and he was the sworn enemy of monotony—what he described as "excessive uniformity in composition and taste." The music compensates for its superabundant thematic variety, as you will hear in the Sonata in C Minor Wq 50/6, by making sure that the ideas are so strongly contrasted and expressively specific that you can always distinguish one from the other. This is key. His melodies might seem odd or difficult to grasp initially, but this is only true when considering them out of their intended context. In their proper place they make the intended effect with often shocking directness and immediacy. His objective, as he explained, was one of "constantly varying the passions." The performer should "barely quiet one before he rouses another." As a threshold matter, you can't very well "vary the passions" without creating thematic material that is highly "passion specific" in the first place.

There's something truly special and audacious in all of this, because Bach certainly had the ability to write simple, singable melodies. Indeed, he composed nearly three hundred songs. Many of them are extremely catchy and they became very popular. He was, moreover, wholly dedicated to the commonly held belief that all instrumental composition aspired to the communicative spirit of vocal music. The very first sonata in his very first published set—the Sonata in F Major, Wq 48/1 (1740), from the "Prussian" Sonatas—contains a slow movement in the style of an operatic recitative, and he marks it as such. During his lifetime, Bach was known as a composer who made his music "speak." So vivid was his ability to build characterful musical phrases into larger monologues and dialogues that one of his contemporaries attached two vocal texts (Hamlet's famous 'To be or not to be" soliloquy and the last utterance of the dying Socrates) to the Fantasia in C Minor, the last movement of the Sonata Wq 63/6. Bach was intrigued, but not terribly impressed.

The Sonata in C Minor, Wq 50/6, up for consideration here, may offer an excellent example of Bach's use of melody, but it also has some special features that you will notice immediately as you listen. Most Bach sonatas have three movements arranged in a fast-slow-fast pattern. This one consists of a single movement that plays for between six and seven minutes. Its form will be familiar to you: ABABA—in short, a rondo with episodes all based on the same material. However, because Bach wishes to emphasize the concept of "varied reprises," the piece has more of a feel of a set of variations on two alternating themes. One (A) is a pathetic melody in C minor, while the other (B) offers a cheerful contrast in C major. This form of alternating major/minor variations became standard operating procedure in the hands of Joseph Haydn, and it culminated in the great adagios of Beethoven's Ninth Symphony and the symphonies of Bruckner and Mahler. It all started here.

In addition to contrasts of key, each of the two themes has a particular structure. The C minor theme is the more complex of the two, both musically and emotionally. It has two parts—call them (lowercase) "ab"—which may not sound very complex, but musically speaking this means that even in its simplest form it lacks a certain large-scale symmetry; and Bach exaggerates this by making the "b" half much longer than the "a" opening. The second half ("b") also falls into two parts, the latter being a variant of the former; and since Bach varies every single repeat, each appearance of tune A takes this rather elaborate form: aa'bb'b''b'''. That makes for a lot of change going on within the tune before we even get to the formal variations later on.

Most themes used in variation movements in the classical period fall into two halves, with both repeated, and this aabb structure, albeit without varied repeats at the start, became quite standard. Typical examples include Paganini's Caprice No. 24 in A Minor for solo violin, so memorably reused by Brahms, Rachmaninov, and countless others for their own variations, or the alternately poetic and hilarious slow movement melody of Haydn's "Surprise" Symphony (No. 94). The only thing that distinguishes Bach's practice here is the already generously embellished presentation of the initial melody, and the unusual degree of internal variation from the first note onward. All of these qualities heighten the music's level of tension and, consequently, its depth of pathos.

Bach's major-key, "B" theme also falls into two halves, both repeated, but its shape is quite different from theme "A." If it had no repeats at all, and using a dash to separate the two halves, it would be a simple "a-ba," but with literal repeats it turns into a somewhat lopsided "aa-baba." This is another extremely common sort of melodic shape quite popular both in variations and many other musical situations. Mozart's famous variation set for keyboard based on the French nursery tune "Ah vous dirai-je, Maman," better known to English speakers as "Twinkle, Twinkle, Little Star," offers one example. The rondo theme from the finale of Haydn's delightful Symphony No. 88 provides another.

With varied repeats, Bach's melody sounds like this: aa'ba''b'a'''. This may not look less complicated than the first theme, but nothing in music imparts a greater feeling of stability then a continued return to a familiar idea, especially in its original key, as happens here. You can even see that the tune's rondolike pattern of alternating phrases looks more balanced. Moreover, the "B" melody itself has a much simpler internal structure than the "A" theme, being built mostly of repetitions of a little four-note rhythmic motive. Bach takes care to preserve this pattern throughout most of the ensuing variations. The result has all of the happiness and sense of contentment that "A" lacks. It's not a nursery tune, but I wouldn't be a bit surprised if it gets lodged in your memory all the same.

Bach made this sonata deliberately easy, relatively speaking. Its textures are spare, often moving in just two parts. There is only a single full chord in both hands, just before the end, where the sudden heavy sonority comes as a big surprise. Most listeners today will not even notice as significant the work's most radical, even revolutionary feature: the alternation between C major and C minor as the variations progress. Before Bach tossed the concept out the window, and even for some time afterward, the art of composition was ruled by an aesthetic doctrine known as the single effect rule. This meant, for instrumental music, that a movement should express one, and only one, emotion or sentiment. It was a concept derived from *opera seria* ("serious opera"), in which the action takes place in the rapid dialogue of the recitatives, after which the plotline freezes so that the singers could come forward and express emotion in an aria representing a single feeling in each main section: love, sorrow, triumph, vengeance, joy, death, disbelief, and so forth.

That at least was the theory. As usual in music, the reality was somewhat different, and we always have to be careful to distinguish between what aestheticians and self-appointed tastemakers wrote, and what composers actually did. There is plenty of emotional range, surprise, and variety in the music of the baroque masters. No composer was less doctrinaire than Handel. Much of what we value in the composers we regard as classical stems from their originality—the degree to which they stand out from the contemporaneous crowd. Still, C. P. E. Bach was the most important composer in his day to articulate a style directly opposed to what had previously been regarded as standard practice, as his very own words at the head of this chapter make clear. Nowadays, we are so used to a large work containing a multitude of contrasting emotions both within and between its different parts that the very idea attracts no special notice.

For Bach, however, as also for his musical disciple in this regard, Haydn, the expressive possibilities of joining together multiple affects in a single piece resulted in a style that positively revels in sudden, unpredictable changes of mood. The two great composers explore this new world of feeling with the enthusiasm and gusto of adventurers first setting foot on virgin territory after a long sea voyage. In the "Reprise" Sonata in C Minor, the minor sounds really, really "minor," while the major is very, very "major." Everything down to the finest detail is designed to strengthen the contrast between the two principal ideas, while the carefully balanced large-scale form theoretically assures a basic level of structural integrity. I say "theoretically" here because this last observation is not entirely without controversy.

In Bach's own day, and even in ours, there are those who argue that his new aesthetic paradigm sacrifices some of the music's overall coherence on the altar of uninhibited emotional expression. Whether this is a valid criticism is difficult to say. Arguing against uninhibited emotional expression in music risks sounding prudish, and Bach cared deeply both about matters of form and correctness of execution. Also,

I tend to distrust "zero sum" arguments in art when they suggest that the presence of one quality necessarily precludes another. No composer who wrote hundreds of pieces can be uniformly great all of the time, and Bach was no exception. In the coming pages, we will have the opportunity to discuss some experiments that he thought it better not to repeat. Nevertheless, he lived at a moment when it was possible to write music whose greatness at least partly lies in its ability to capture and transmit to its listeners the wonder and innocent delight in a new discovery. You've had a sample, and now we have much more to consider.

Part 2

Orchestral Music

3 The Concertos—All Fifty-Two of Them

General Introduction

C. P. E. Bach's fifty-two concertos for keyboard and orchestra constitute a body of work fully comparable to such iconic series as Haydn's symphonies or Mozart's piano concertos. They are certainly as rewarding and masterful, yet, the vast majority of them remain unknown. Only nine were published in Bach's lifetime under his personal supervision because the cost of printing scores and parts was prohibitively expensive, especially for works meant more for professional performing organizations rather than the much larger domestic music market. It wasn't until the 1990s that a record label, Sweden's BIS Records, began and completed an extensive project with Hungarian keyboardist Miklós Spányi to record the entire set, including the sonatinas for keyboard and orchestra as well.

That undertaking, now complete, has produced mixed results, as might be expected when dealing with a large volume of unfamiliar work. In terms of sheer musical value it has proven revelatory, but at the same time Spányi's own interpretive quirks, particularly his unwillingness to play some of Bach's allegros with the necessary quickness, rob the music of impact and leave listeners treading water until something better comes along. Still, the important thing is that all of this music is now readily available, and with the Packard Humanities Institute's Complete Works Edition making the scores and parts accessible to performers, we can look forward to at least some of these magnificent pieces returning to the active repertoire of pianists and historical performance specialists in concert and on recordings.

Many of these works exist in multiple versions, for keyboard as well as for different solo instruments. In the latter form a few of them have retained a tenuous foothold in the repertoire historically: three concertos for flute or cello, another two for flute, two for oboe, and two for organ. In most of these cases a version for melody instrument represents the original, with the keyboard transcription coming later, but all are equally valid. Comparison between them, as you might expect, makes for some fascinating listening. Thus far, recordings of the concertos for flute and cello have been particularly abundant owing to the scarcity of major works for those instruments. Bach's contributions, particularly the cello concertos, easily rank with the best eighteenth-century pieces for their respective solos.

In revising an existing concerto for a different instrument, Bach retained the orchestral score virtually unaltered, but wrote an entirely new part in idiomatic style for the featured soloist. He was in any case always prepared to tinker with the solo and orchestral parts over time, adding winds (usually horns and flutes) to the basic string ensemble, and writing down several dozen of his own theoretically improvised cadenzas so as not to leave his music at the mercy of less than tasteful soloists. This practice speaks volumes about his compositional approach, both as regards the fluidity of his ever-variable melodies, as well as the essential details of his concerto forms.

Credit for the invention of the keyboard concerto usually goes to J. S. Bach, and in particular to his Brandenburg Concerto No. 5 (ca. 1719), which actually features three soloists: harpsichord, flute, and violin. However, the monster cadenza for solo keyboard that Bach Sr. included in the first movement effectively diminishes the importance of the other two featured instruments. The idea of using the keyboard as the protagonist in a concerto otherwise only took off in the 1730s, but if you look at the timeline you will note that the first true solo concerto for keyboard may not have been composed by Bach the father, but rather by C. P. E., in 1733. With but a single exception (the Concerto for Two Harpsichords in C Major, BWV 1061), none of the elder Bach's keyboard concertos started life as a work for that medium.

Bach's keyboard concertos represent a fresh and exciting exploration of a genuinely new medium. They cover his entire career, the first of them being composed when he was just nineteen, and the last in the year of his death, 1788, at age seventy-four. Lasting anywhere from twelve minutes to nearly half an hour, none of them is a minor work in terms of either musical quality or expressive depth, and more than a few are flat-out masterpieces. Best of all, if you find the sound of the harpsichord aurally fatiguing in large quantities—and you wouldn't be alone—then you can enjoy some of the best of them played on the piano, the cello, the flute, the oboe, and even the organ.

In the following discussion I propose to describe all of them individually, but briefly, and I refer you to Table 1 listing Bach's complete concerted works in all of their various versions so you can see the big picture. After considering the concertos, in the next chapter we will also take a look at the sonatinas for keyboard and orchestra, a rather generic name for a medium invented entirely by C. P. E. Bach, and adopted by no one else since.

Table 1: Concertos and Sonatinas with Orchestra

Wq #	Key	Alternate Version(s)	Wq or H #
	Concertos for Keyboard		
1	A minor		
2	E-flat major		
3	G major		
4	G major		
5	C minor		
6	G minor		
7	A major		
8	A major		
9	G major		
10	B-flat major		
11	D major		
12	F major		
13	D major		
14	E major		
15	E minor		

continued

Wq #	Key	Alternate Version(s)	Wq or H #
16	G major		
17	D minor		
18	D major		
19	A major		
20	C major		
21	A minor		
22	D minor	Flute	H 484/1
23	D minor		
24	E minor		
25	B-flat major		
26	A minor	Flute	Wq 166
	A minor	Cello	Wq 170
27	D major		
28	B-flat major	Flute	Wq 167
	B-flat major	Cello	Wq 171
29	A major	Flute	Wq 168
	A major	Cello	Wq 172
30	B minor		
31	C minor		
32	G minor		
33	F major		
34	G major	Flute	Wq 169
	G major	Organ (same Wq #)	
35	E-flat major	Organ (same Wq #)	
36	B-flat major		
37	C minor		
38	F major		
39	B-flat major	Oboe	Wq 164
40	E-flat major	Oboe	Wq 165
41	E-flat major		
42	F major	Solo Keyboard version	
43	Nos. 1–6 as below		

continued

Wq #	Key	Alternate Version(s)	Wq or H #
	No. 1 in F major	Solo Keyboard version	H 471
	No. 2 in D major	Solo Keyboard version	H 472
	No. 3 in E-flat major	Solo Keyboard version	H 473
	No. 4 in C minor	Solo Keyboard version	H 474
	No. 5 in G major	Solo Keyboard version	H 475
	No. 6 in C major	Solo Keyboard version	H 476
44	G major		
45	D major		
46	F-major (2 harpsichords)		
47	E-flat major (harpsichord and piano)		
Sonatinas for Keyboard and Orchestra			
96	D major		
97	G major		
98	G major		
99	F major		
100	E major		
101/106	C major		
102	D major		
103	C major		
104/107	D minor		
105/108	E-flat major		
109	D major (2 harpsichords)		
110	B-flat major (2 harpsichords)		

The concerto form that Bach inherited from his father, and stuck with all of his life, grew out of the operatic aria. An orchestral introduction sets up the entrance of the singer and returns periodically to punctuate the presentation of the words, giving the soloist a chance to breathe, and theoretically deepening the expressive intensity of the musical message. This introduction is called a ritornello, which we have already met in the last chapter in connection with the rondo, a very similar form. That's basically all there is to it. The only other thing you need to know about ritornello form, as it came to be called, is that the internal repetitions of the main theme take the music through different keys while its last appearance returns to the home key to convey a feeling of finality and closure.

Bach's strategy, however, hardly reflects a stubborn allegiance to an outmoded aesthetic. It's worth pointing out that to the extent all concertos display a regular alternating pattern of solo and orchestral episodes, they all use some kind of ritornello form, whatever it may have come to be called later. It's simply the natural and obvious thing to do. The standard version in Bach's day contained, in a typical quick movement, three solo episodes and four statements of the ritornello, but it's important to realize that several factors will influence the listener's perception of what actually happens as the music plays.

First, there is the question of whether the solo enters with the theme of the ritornello, has new and independent material, or some combination of each. This has a direct expressive impact: it can produce the impression of cooperation or opposition between solo and orchestra, and every degree in between. Think of the two parties as independent personalities and listen to how the music characterizes them. To draw a useful analogy, musical scholars today often speak of Verdi's operatic duets as falling into two types: "similar," in which the protagonists are of the same mind (and often music), and "dissimilar," where they confront each other with different points of view. Bach's concertos, while more subtle and abstract on account of the lack of text, operate in much the same way.

Second, while the solo may play alone in the allegedly "solo" episodes, the orchestra will often accompany, interrupt, and otherwise participate in dialogue, and in Bach's music the keyboard may also accompany the orchestra with its continuo part. So, the divisions between solo and tutti (when the full orchestra plays) need not be carved in stone. However, the solo will indeed play by itself in any passage consisting of a cadenza, a moment in which the player gets to improvise based on the themes heard so far. As previously mentioned,

Bach wrote a bunch of these down so as not to place his music entirely at the mercy of the player. Mozart also composed numerous cadenzas for his piano concertos, and Beethoven, in his "Emperor" Concerto, eliminated the improvised cadenza entirely. So, for that matter, did Bach in the six concertos of Wq 43.

Traditionally, the cadenza occurs in connection with the final solo appearance, just before the orchestra wraps up the movement with the ritornello, but Bach may place one or more at various points within a movement. There really are no rules about this; it depends on the work, and it's a mistake to assume that because Bach uses ritornello form in his concertos, they all have the same shape or structure. A better way to think about it would be to say that Bach adopts the ritornello *principle* so as to give each concerto its own unique form. No two works are identical, and discovering how the solo and orchestra interact expressively makes listening to the music a particularly rewarding experience.

The key, then, in listening to any concerto movement by Bach is this: *know the ritornello.* It can be long or short, slow or fast, of any expressive temper, and consist of broadly lyrical melodies or a number of short, punchy motives, in any combination. The ritornello immediately announces the terms of the ensuing discourse, and goes a long way toward determining the shape of a movement. Bach's ritornellos contain some of the most straightforwardly catchy, unforgettable ideas that he ever concocted, alternating with his most dazzling keyboard writing. The concertos thus offer a world of truly gripping music.

Wq 23 in D Minor (1748)

We begin our consideration of the concertos with Wq 23 because it is included in the audio tracks that come with this book, and because in-depth discussion provides the key that unlocks a gateway to the remaining works. This concerto, written in 1748, had the good fortune to be published at the beginning of the twentieth century, and so it became the most familiar of all of Bach's efforts in the medium. It is unquestionably one of his greatest pieces, but writers who label it the "best" generally do so without having heard many of the others.

It also makes an apt companion on recordings to J. S. Bach's greatest keyboard concerto, BWV 1052, also in D minor. The piece has three movements, is scored for keyboard and strings, and plays for about twenty-two minutes.

First Movement: Allegro

Ritornello I

Played by strings alone in this performance (which features a modern piano), the long opening contains a large number of distinctive motives. The very opening bars contain two very striking and memorable gestures: an initial falling octave, and a trill, all in jagged, dotted rhythm. *Dotted* simply means a short note followed by a long one, and describes the musical notation used to indicate the appropriate rhythm. If you say the phrase "Time to go," you will naturally produce a dotted rhythm: "Dum, daDum," because the word "to" will be shorter and less strongly accented than "time" or "go." This sort of rhythm, then, is a natural concurrent of speech, and Bach uses it very frequently in contrast to other, more equal or smooth kinds of rhythmic movement.

The ensuing melody consists of very wide skips and leaps, and it never appears exactly the same way twice, but its shape is so memorable that you always know it whenever it reappears. It is immediately followed by a quiet "echo" that stops the music's surging momentum, but only for a moment. Continuing those sharp, dotted rhythms with stubbornly repeated melodic fragments over a motoric repeated-note accompaniment, the ritornello drives to a close with a series of dramatic lunges from the violins. This leads to:

The First Solo

The piano enters with the opening motive of the ritornello, and then orchestra and solo parcel out the continuation between them in varied form. The solo then embarks on a long digression accompanied softly by the strings, gently working its way back to the later bit of the ritornello, but only for a moment. Bach has a surprise for us in the form of a cadenza (fully composed, not improvised): the orchestra stops and the piano plays a rhapsodic interlude based on the motives of the ritornello, and with this the first solo concludes, leading back to:

Ritornello II

I mentioned that during the first solo, the piano extended the middle section with new material. Bach has clearly singled out this bit for special handling. This next version of the ritornello begins with an almost literal repeat of the opening, but varies the music yet again by leaving out that original middle section entirely, jumping instead to the ritornello's closing phrases, so as to return swiftly to:

The Second Solo

This long section covers a very wide range of contrasts. In later music it would be considered the formal "development section" of a movement in sonata form, because in it the composer explores all of the different expressive things he can do with his material, and introduces new ideas for the soloist besides. There is much close dialogue between the orchestra and the piano—Bach was a very great master at this sort of swift byplay—with bits of the ritornello constantly returning and leading to arresting new developments.

Ritornello III

The abbreviated version of the ritornello returns, slightly varied once again, introducing:

The Third Solo

This is an entirely new episode for the piano, featuring brilliant figuration accompanied softly by the orchestra. After an unconvincing reappearance of the ritornello's opening in a bright major key (that's why it's unconvincing), the orchestra finally bursts in with:

Ritornello IV

To give the necessary feeling of finality as well as fulfill the demands of the concerto as a work for both solo and orchestra, Bach returns not to the ritornello as it originally appeared, but to the version the two protagonists shared in the first solo, combining the proprietary elements of both. This means you get the solo's initial digression, plus the entire original middle section—decorated by the piano—plus the written-out cadenza, all varied and elaborated, leading after the cadenza to the final phrases of the ritornello (instead of to its return, as previously) and so on to the close.

When you have a first solo that discusses the ritornello in dialogue with the orchestra and incorporates new material of its own, alongside an extended recapitulation such as this, we are now very close to the standard, classical period first movement concerto form with double exposition that you may have learned in music appreciation classes or read about in textbooks. The major difference between the two comes from the presence of that third ritornello/solo complex, which gives the movement more of a rondo character. In subsequent music this was absorbed into a longer, more tonally goal-directed development section, producing the exposition-development-recapitulation/coda structure with which we are most familiar.

This is one reason that Bach came to be regarded as the most important forerunner of the Viennese classics, but as you can plainly hear, his own practice can't be thought of as primitive or in any way underdeveloped. It gives him as subtle and sophisticated a means of articulating the music's expressive message as anything that came later. Formal patterns, as with any tool, depend far less on what theoretical shape they take than on how well the artist knows how to use them. With his father as his teacher and example, allied to his own intelligence and imagination, Bach certainly knew what he was about.

Second Movement: Poco andante (slightly slow)

The form of this Andante (and the finale too) is basically the same as that of the first movement, but it's actual shape feels quite different, and rather than give you a blow by blow description it's easier to speak of the music's mood and temperament. What really happens here is that Bach offers a dialogue between the piano and the orchestra that grows steadily more passionate as the movement proceeds. In his concertos based in minor keys for the two outer quick movements, the central slow part will often be in a contrasting major, and the opposite is the case for concertos rooted in major keys. It's all part of Bach's strategy to maximize contrast between sections.

Sounding as if it began in midsentence, the initial ritornello is quite short, with a touch of nostalgia to it. The solo enters right away with a lyrical tune that gets interrupted by dotted-rhythmic exclamations from the full orchestra. These kinds of orchestral interjections are very typical of the kind of thing we hear in operatic recitative, and you may well imagine either a conversation between two characters, or a long monologue running through widely different moods, featuring lyrical meditations interrupted by a number of passionate exclamations. The more the orchestra gets involved, the more agitated and pathetic the soloist becomes. This, essentially, is the story that the music tells, and I leave further details to your imagination.

Finale: Allegro assai (Very quick)

Most concertos, including many by C. P. E. Bach and most from the classical period, feature finales distinctly lighter and more relaxed in tone than the earlier movements. This one is less complex simply by virtue of its relative brevity, but it is also the most intense part of the entire work—a furious whirlwind of a piece that caps the whole concerto with an unforgettable conclusion. The first thing you will notice about the ritornello is that it shares many of the same features as the start of the first movement: the initial drop of an octave, the trill, and those swooning leaps in the violins. It's all of a piece, and an important example of Bach's tendency to think of a work whole, as a single continuous thought, however much contrast and variety we encounter from start to finish. This quality remains one of the music's most progressive features, and we will encounter it often in Bach's work.

The opening motive, which contains six notes as played in the orchestra and seven when the piano takes it up, is omnipresent, and binds the movement together in an iron grip. Even so, both orchestra and piano have music unique to themselves: the orchestra, for example, has a motive consisting of repeated rhythmic cells that grind along like some sort of evil machine. The solo, for its part, starts out playing the ritornello, and then shrugs it off in favor of entirely new material. Otherwise, the opening motive acts both as theme as well as accompaniment virtually throughout the movement. It is extraordinary music that you won't readily find in the work of any other composer.

One aspect of Bach's ritornello form may take some getting used to if you're familiar with later, classical or romantic concertos. Because most movements will end with the ritornello, the music doesn't build to a big, flashy conclusion in the way that came later. In performances where the soloist also performs the continuo part, everyone will at least play together up to the last bar, and Bach's method has an undeniable logical severity that, in works such as the D Minor Concerto, certainly lacks nothing in finality—whether cheerful or, as here, grim. However, the fact that the music has no need for an extended coda means that the ending can arrive with surprising abruptness even compared to earlier works (such as J. S. Bach's) that also use ritornello form.

The reason for this, I believe, stems from the unusually high level of energy that C. P. E.'s music generates, resulting in the feeling that it sometimes wants to keep on going past the point where it actually stops. This is, obviously, a very subjective impression, but I think a valid one. Bach exploits this tendency dramatically in works such as the Hamburg symphonies (and other pieces) where all of the movements are played continuously, and he can make one interrupt another with often shocking suddenness. In the concertos, suffice it to say that the big moments for the soloist tend to occur somewhere in the middle of a movement rather than at the very end; and, of course, it's always better for a piece to leave you wanting more rather than running on for too long.

Fifty-Two Concertos

Three Early Concertos

Bach's three early keyboard concertos, along with those of his father dating from roughly the same period, basically represent the earliest examples that we have of the form. During this period, J. S. Bach was director of the Leipzig Collegium Musicum, which gave regular concerts at Zimmermann's Coffee House. Composed primarily of university students and other semiprofessionals, the programs provided an excellent opportunity to showcase the talents of the entire Bach family, and C. P. E.'s three concertos of the 1730s reveal no youthful hesitation or uncertainty whatsoever. Part of the reason doubtless stems from the fact that he revised them all in the 1740s for performances in Berlin, but even so it's undeniable that he had both talent and originality from the very start of his career.

Wq 1 in A Minor (1733, rev. 1744)

Bach was only nineteen years old when he composed this piece. The opening ritornello features a singularly "dark" use of the minor key that C. P. E. probably learned from his father, whose use of minor keys often sounds similarly grim. The slow movement begins with a very long ritornello, and has the character of an aria in which the keyboard and orchestra engage in close dialogue. Bach asks that the finale be played very quickly (allegro assai). The music is violent and vigorous in a way that his dad never dreamed of. The solo's initial entrance is rhythmically tricky and the part generally is very flashy, with lots of fast passagework in triplet rhythms.

Wq 2 in E-flat Major (1734, rev. 1743)

The opening ritornello, although nominally in the home key of E-flat major, has a tendency to drift into minor keys, spicing up the harmonic palette and deepening the expressive range. In the Adagio we meet a *topos*, or "topic," to which Bach will return very frequently: gruff exclamations from the orchestra in jerky, dotted rhythms alternating with more songlike phrases. When the solo enters, it takes over the melodic passages while the orchestra continues with its rude interruptions. This formula is very characteristic of operatic recitative, and it creates a vivid dialogue between the soloist and the orchestra. Bach was a master of this style, which culminated in the very famous slow movement of Beethoven's Fourth Piano Concerto, also scored for keyboard and strings alone. The finale, again, is very quick, with a wacky principal theme full of unexpected twists and turns.

Wq 3 in G Major (1737, rev. 1743)

Bach's music in the key of G major usually has a particularly sunny, even rustic quality, enhanced in this case by ritornello's syncopated rhythms. The first movement features the soloist and orchestra in close dialogue, while the minor-key slow movement gives us something very different than what we heard in Wq 2: the principal theme (really just a rhythmic pattern more than a tune) leads off loudly, interrupted by quiet, gentler phrases. The lack of clearly defined melody means that the keyboard needs independent material, so that's just what Bach provides, although if you listen closely you'll find that the rhythmic pattern of the opening has now become the accompaniment to the solo. In this manner, you can hear how Bach adapts just a few simple elements to a variety of expressive purposes. The finale is in triple time, and has a vigorous rhythmic swing as well as one of those rising, chromatic bass lines that you can also hear in "L'Aly Rupalich."

The Berlin Concertos

For the next thirty years Bach lived and worked at the court of Frederick the Great in Berlin, and during this time he composed thirty-seven concertos—more if we take into account revisions of the three early works and the individual versions for various instruments of some of the newer ones. This is an extremely impressive legacy, particularly if we consider that, to the best of our knowledge, these pieces were not composed for Bach's royal patron, who disliked his music generally. The existence of these works does, however, point to a rich musical culture in Berlin society the evidence for which, as you will see, we find in commissions that Bach continued to receive from music-loving patrons in Berlin long after he had left the city for Hamburg.

Frederick's sister, Princess Anna Amalia, for example, owned numerous C. P. E. Bach compositions, and made him her honorary *Kapellmeister* (music director) on his departure from Berlin in 1768. Bach also cultivated friendships with noted members of the German Enlightenment, including the Jewish philosopher Moses Mendelssohn; playwright Gotthold Ephraim Lessing; and the philosopher Johann Georg Sulzer, whose *General Theory of the Fine Arts* (1771–74) became one of the signal books on aesthetics published in the second half of the eighteenth century. In other words, Bach enjoyed a large, influential, and highly educated circle of friends, one that certainly would have appreciated challenging new music, had the resources on hand to perform it well, and undoubtedly encouraged him to maintain the consistently high standard that we find in these concertos.

Wq 4 in G Major (1738)

Bach's first concerto for his new Berlin friends and patrons features generally harmonious cooperation between the solo and the orchestra. The two share much of the thematic material in a gracious dialogue. Perhaps the most striking movement is the finale, which has that freshness peculiar to Bach's music in G major, interrupted only by a sudden, dissonant excursion to a minor key. Does the music's relative conservatism show Bach getting his bearings in his new surroundings? You be the judge.

Wq 5 in C Minor (1739, rev. 1762)

A tendency to make revisions generally means that Bach either had a special affection for a particular piece, or that he felt a need to adapt it to changing tastes and circumstances (or both). This C Minor Concerto definitely goes in for expressive depth, although not at the expense of virtuosity. The opening ritornello is lyrical and moody, while the entrance of the solo features some ear-catching, odd dissonances. Bach gives away his intentions in the slow movement by marking it "Arioso," that is, a vocal piece, and he obviously intends that it be played as songfully as possible. The melody includes tiny echoes of a romantic character, as well as pauses for dramatic effect. The finale, marked "Allegro spirituoso," like the first movement is not terribly quick. It recaptures the dark mood of the opening while striving to retain something of the Arioso's lyricism.

Wq 6 in G Minor (1740)

Another concerto in a minor key, this one has a long, sad ritornello with many drops to a soft (piano) dynamic along the way. The work's center of gravity however is the Largo, the longest movement in the piece, offering a very beautiful hymnlike theme that retains something of the first movement's sadness even though the key is major rather than minor. In the finale, Bach maintains the music's seriousness by avoiding any suggestion of the dance. The tempo, however, is very quick, the rhythm strong with slashing accents and plenty of characterful interplay between the solo and the orchestra. All in all this is a very moving and powerful work.

Wq 7 in A Major (1740)

The first movement of this concerto is particularly virtuosic, with a bold ritornello that dips for a moment into a soft, minor key before resuming the bright opening texture and dynamic. The entrance of the solo is brilliant, featuring big, full chords that demand an instrument with a large tone—not always something you can count on with a harpsichord. Bach gives the solo most of the thematic interest in the slow movement, and evokes the dance in a triple-time finale that has a welcome degree of rhythmic swing.

Wq 8 in A Major (1741)

Bach stays in A major for this concerto, a relatively short (about twenty minutes or less), intimate piece. The first movement's ritornello is gentle, with a sudden, sad moment, but a vigorous conclusion. When the solo enters it engages in plenty of back-and-forth dialogue with the orchestra. Bach marks the slow movement "Andante e con sordini," that is, "with mutes" on the strings, further emphasizing the music's delicacy and Italian-style lyricism. The weight of the piece, at least as concerns its energy level, lies in the vigorous finale, with its sturdy syncopations and unbuttoned vitality.

Wq 9 in G Major (1742)

As you may have noticed, Bach liked G major, a tonality relatively easy to play in. It has only one "accidental" (F-sharp) in its scale and so stays mostly on what we would now call the white keys of the instrument. As noted previously, Bach seems to have associated G major with the sort of hearty, good-humored gusto that characterizes the opening ritornello of this concerto. The dotted rhythms here sound perky rather than gruff, and the solo takes advantage of a sudden drop in tempo for more reflective, improvisational passages. It also gets more harmonically adventurous as the movement proceeds. The slow movement is gently nostalgic and not too sad, while the finale recaptures the vigor of the first movement, urged on by emphatic chords for the full string orchestra.

Wq 10 in B-flat Major (1742)

This is a delightful work, rich in humor as well as lyrical substance. The ritornello is very pithy, and consists of short phrases with witty pauses here and there for emphasis. This permits a particularly close dialogue between the solo and the orchestra throughout the movement. The minor-key Largo presents us with a very poignant, expressive melody over a flowing triplet accompaniment. Bach saves much of the fun for the finale: a rugged Presto, ma non troppo (very fast, but not too much) in which some of the "non troppo" parts consist of sustained, mysterious echoes, while the strings in the more boisterous moments rudely interrupt the solo, trying to throw it off-kilter.

Wq 11 in D Major (1743)

Bach published this concerto, and in one early source it exists with trumpet and timpani parts that scholars believe to be inauthentic (the Complete Works Edition leaves them out, as does Bach's Estate Catalog). The BIS recording includes them nevertheless. Their relentless fanfares tend to make the music sound more foursquare than it otherwise would, but the huge contrasts in texture and dynamics are still fun to hear. D major is, in any case, a celebratory key because it was ideally suited to brass instruments in the days before valves enhanced their utility, and this is unquestionably a festive piece, with flashy solo parts in the quick outer movements and tunes of genuine, popular appeal. It's also a big work, around twenty-five minutes long. The very slow Adagio di molto, on the other hand, exploits the low sonorities of the strings to ominous effect, creating the largest possible contrast to the rest of the concerto. A "public" piece, then, but not one that panders to lesser tastes.

Wq 12 in F Major (1744)

Both in this work and the previous D Major Concerto, Bach seems to have been trying to create an unusually strong contrast between vivacious outer movements and very slow, sad central slow movements. This one is marked "Largo e sostenuto" (very slow and sustained), and it is very dark indeed, almost grim. It features those signature dotted rhythms mentioned in connection with Wq 2, but the mood is more tragic. The outer movements couldn't be more different: the opening ritornello has an infectious vigor conveyed by its steady rhythmic motion, and both here and in the finale the keyboard writing sounds especially flashy and brilliant. Bach gives the solo plenty of new material in the first two movements, but the keyboard joins the orchestra harmoniously in the finale, sharing the tunes equally.

Wq 13 in D Major (1744)

This opening ritornello is really fun. It features repeated notes that tend to go off in all kinds of directions, interspersed with more reflective bits. Bach gives the solo new material entirely, but then begins to insinuate some of those sneaky repeated-note figurations. The slow movement is highly unpredictable and irregular, with lots of dynamic variation, while the main theme of the finale wants to wander off into minor keys before being pulled firmly back to D major for the entrance of the solo. The ensuring dialogue is especially brisk. This is a very different work from the previous concerto in D major: wittier, quirkier, and wider in expressive range within its movements, rather than between them.

Wq 14 in E Major (1744)

Bach published this concerto in 1760, and some sources include possibly inauthentic horn parts. The Complete Works Edition omits them. This is another big, public concerto, and you might argue that it does indeed offer "more sugar" than some of Bach's other works in the form. The opening ritornello is broad and unusually smooth, but it has a real expansiveness of phrasing that's very striking. The music soars. The solo enters with the same theme, and no wonder. The central Poco adagio, on the other hand, is very dramatic. It has a slithery main theme that incorporates sudden, grinding dissonances. If this movement has extra sugar, then it's added to sweeten the lemonade. A steady rhythm keeps the music flowing forward as the solo takes up the main theme. The finale starts with a rollicking opening followed by a highly contrasted, harmonically ambiguous answer. The ritornello is long enough to have a distinct, ABA shape, and the solo shares the tune with the orchestra in a witty dialogue. Pay particular attention to the moment where that reflective bit comes back in the solo, and things really get interesting.

Wq 15 in E Minor (1745)

Here we have another large concerto, about twenty-five minutes long. The opening Allegro is extremely agitated, and the solo has an absolutely wonderful, grand entrance full of dramatic hesitations, sweeping keyboard gestures, and abrupt interjections from the orchestra. This is music with a huge personality, and it's a pity that it took until 1996 for a recording to appear. In stark contrast to the first movement, the Adagio is mellow and lyrical, and some of this spills over into the finale, with its compact ritornello. Despite even more very flamboyant and romantic keyboard writing, the solo and orchestra cooperate closely in bringing the work to an extremely satisfying conclusion.

Wq 16 in G Major (1745)

The first movement's ritornello exudes that open-air freshness that we so often find in Bach's use of G major, and the solo enters with the tune in the left hand. It has a simple, folklike quality made more fetching by the colorful pizzicato accompaniment. In the ensuing Adagio assai, with its very songful main theme, Bach retains the major key—unusually for a work of this period—but the music also features lots of chromaticism (notes foreign to the home tonality), with a decided turn toward minor keys and dissonant harmony. The Allegretto finale is a gutsy movement with bold syncopations in its rhythm. It's actually a bigger piece than the comparatively relaxed first movement. This is very different than what we usually find in the later, classical concerto with its steady pattern of relaxation as the music proceeds. Because Bach uses similar forms in the outer movements, the concerto's balance can be shifted to the finale relatively easily, the only major consideration being overall length and the music's emotional progression.

Wq 17 in D Minor (1745)

This is not a particularly dark D minor. The opening melody has an arresting, driving energy, with wide leaps in its thematic material, but it has a tendency to "go major," and the solo's personality is even more amiable. The slow movement, Un poco adagio, starts in a sweet and serene major key, but does just the opposite of what we heard in the first movement: it wants to "go minor," with interruptions in Bach's patented dotted notes. Notice how lilting these rhythms become when taken up by the soloist in a major key—a wonderful transformation, and a really beautiful movement in general. The finale's ritornello is very tense, and the solo uses the opening motive obsessively both as melody as well as accompaniment. This kind of motivic work became a very important element of the classical style, and of much later music too.

Wq 18 in D Major (1745)

The first movement has a gracious, courtly quality that probably ought to be called "rococo," except that the solo's rising chromatic bass lines undermine the music's good manners. Pay particular attention to what happens in the soloist's left hand, to get the full measure of Bach's sly humor. The Andante moves in slow triplets with a melody not too distant from J. S. Bach's famous "Jesu, joy of man's desiring," and the finale is catchy with more than a touch of harmonic spice to keep the music vibrant. This isn't C. P. E.'s most distinctive concerto, but its lower emotional temperature doesn't mean that the work is any less well crafted than we have come to expect.

Wq 19 in A Major (1746)

Bach opens this concerto with a gentle and elegant ritornello, allegretto, with a syncopated rhythm to add a touch of additional interest. The solo and orchestra reveal very different characters over the course of the movement, with the solo comparatively reflective and the orchestra more animated. Hearing this music, we begin to understand that the expressive point is more important to Bach than mere virtuosity, although he never forgets that, either. The slow movement is an elegiac Andante, and some sources allow a solo flute to double the violins, while the joyful finale has a distinctive "classical" flavor without really being classical; perhaps it's those typical C. P. E.-style interruptions. It's almost the sort of thing we hear much later from a composer like Poulenc (*Concert champêtre*)—but that wouldn't happen until the twentieth century.

Wq 20 in C Major (1746)

There's no tempo indication for the first movement, which isn't as odd as it may sound. Most of the time the basic speed will be evident from the character of the music, and this piece is clearly an allegro. It's one of the longest movements in any Bach concerto, and it contains a singularly wacky ritornello that includes phrases of every length, tonality, dynamic, rhythm, unexpected pauses—you name it. The result when the soloist enters is a fascinating and totally unpredictable dialogue. In the following Adagio ma non troppo, Bach provides a heartfelt movement of contrasting minor key, romantic expressive intensity. The very quick finale starts with another highly diverse ritornello containing a particularly evocative minor-key digression. As in the first movement, an abundance of musical phrases and shapes permits a kaleidoscopic dialogue between the solo and the orchestra. All in all, this is one of Bach's most distinctive concertos—and it wasn't recorded for the first time until 2003.

Wq 21 in A Minor (1747, rev. 1775)

A beautiful and intimate piece, the mood is not angry or "crazy" for all that the key is A minor, but it is uneasy. Perhaps "pathetic" describes it best. The first movement is highly conversational, with the keyboard and orchestra sharing material and discussing it between them. The Adagio is a solemn, ethereal piece in the major, in which a stern unison leads to a serene meditation. Bach really cuts loose in the finale, a genuine Sturm und Drang (storm and stress) allegro whose broken phrases may strike you as somewhat similar to the finale of Wq 23.

Wq 22 in D Minor (1747)

This piece also exists as a flute concerto, H 484/1, although Bach's authorship is doubtful and Wotquenne did not mention it. Some of the rhapsodic writing for the solo over sustained strings points to the possibility of a wind instrument rather than the keyboard as being original, but it's lovely either way. Despite the minor key, the very lyrical ritornello features broad phrases more warmly expressive than menacing. The central Poco andante is a hymnlike, solemn, sustained essay in song, once again rich and generous in feeling. That changes with the Allegro di molto finale, a wild ride that has all of the angst and tension we expect of D minor.

Wq 23 in D Minor (1748, already discussed at the start of this chapter)

Wq 24 in E Minor (1748)

This interesting concerto features two Allegrettos framing a central Largo. It's another big piece, around twenty-five minutes or more. The pulsating rhythm of the first movement, almost like a ticking clock, has a certain relentless quality, especially when the solo picks it up. Bach seldom asks for such rhythmic uniformity, but his idea comes into focus in the Largo, which is shorter than both outer movements and full of abrupt pauses and sudden outbursts. While asking for the same speed as the opening, the finale is palpably more energetic, and once again features short, highly varied phrases that are perfect for close dialogue and sudden exchanges between the solo and orchestra.

Wq 25 in B-flat Major (1749)

One of the three individual works that C. P. E. Bach published personally, this is another bold, "public" work, but it is also a very characteristic one. The very energetic opening, Allegro di molto, contains a slew of memorable gestures, sudden dynamic shifts, and abrupt accents. It confirms that major keys can be every bit as intense as minor ones. In fact, this ritornello is notably compact, and its high level of incident means an abundance of whiplash exchanges between the solo and the orchestra. The Largo mesto (very slow and sad) movement is tragic in tone, the aching chromatic harmony punctuated by sudden, more consoling phrases. The notation here is incredibly detailed, with strings both muted and unmuted, and dynamics often differentiated between individual notes. The tempo designation for the finale, Prestissimo, basically says it all. It should be played as quickly as humanly possible (the BIS recording unfortunately doesn't). The sharp accents for the strings obviously recall the similar writing in the first movement. A very great and hugely entertaining work.

With this work we come to the end of the series of concertos that Bach completed during the lifetime of his father—twenty-six works in all (including the Double Concerto, Wq 46, which is out of order in Wotquenne's catalog). The reasons I stress this point repeatedly are: first, I find the overlapping of styles between the two to be fascinating in its own right; and second, it drives home the point that some of the newness of the music—which we can't recapture today, unfortunately—stems from the mere fact that C. P. E. devoted so much time and attention to the medium of the keyboard concerto, which was wholly novel in the 1730s and '40s. Indeed, it was something of a Bach family specialty: their gift to future generations of musicians and music lovers.

Wq 26 in A Minor (1750)

This piece probably originated as a cello concerto, and in that form it has become quite popular with good reason. It is quite possibly the finest cello concerto written in the eighteenth century, although the flute and keyboard arrangements are also impressive and gaining ground. The opening ritornello presents an instantly memorable five-note motive that permeates the first movement, either on the surface or as a persistent accompaniment. This gives the music an obsessive quality that, combined with the dashing string writing and syncopated rhythmic figures, creates and sustains an amazing level of tension. The solo writing, often of great urgency and virtuosity, doesn't hurt either. For the slow movement Bach offers a very songful Andante in an expressive major key, albeit one with strong minor leanings. Both outer movements are marked "Allegro assai," and like the Concerto in D Minor, Wq 23, the main theme of the finale is clearly related to that of the first movement. If you enjoyed Wq 23, you'll love this concerto just as much.

Wq 27 in D Major (1750)

The engaging and vigorous ritornello of the first movement turns out to be quite independent of the first solo, which takes the music in some startling new directions. There's a real sense of two unique personalities here, although their interactions are more genial than they are confrontational. Bach calls the slow movement a siciliana, a graceful Italian dance with a very lyrical main theme and a touch of pathos thanks to its minor key. The finale starts off with jagged unisons and broken phrases familiar from the finale of Wq 23, but the mood is completely different. The ritornello is long and extremely varied, while the solo enters with even more new material before taking on the ritornello in dialogue with the orchestra. Whereas the music of Wq 23 produced a sense of great compactness, Bach's strategy here highlights the grander scale of the piece.

Wq 28 in B-flat Major (1751)

As in Wq 26, this concerto exists in three versions: for cello, flute, and keyboard. It couldn't be more different from its predecessor. The opening ritornello is short, gracious, and quite "rococo." It turns out to be the start of a highly conversational dialogue with the soloist, one that constantly varies the theme as it proceeds. However, this relatively innocuous opening turns out to be deceptive as an indicator of what's coming: the long main theme of the central Adagio contains some very striking dissonances. It sounds almost irate, albeit with a gentler, more pleasing second strain and a sudden flurry of notes at the end. The finale, too, is more intense that the first movement. A very quick Allegro assai, it contains some very ear-catching and abrupt moments. The interjections from the soloist toward the end of its first entrance are particularly witty. This is another work where the focus is on the finale rather than the first movement.

Wq 29 in A Major (1753)

Here is the last concerto that Bach arranged for cello, flute, and keyboard, and like its brethren it probably started out as a cello concerto. The opening ritornello is very diverse for its size, and it introduces a movement in closely argued dialogue, with some very virtuosic solo writing and sudden orchestral outbursts. Whenever the composer uses a very slow tempo designation in his concertos, as in this Largo molto, we can be almost completely sure that it means a very dark and deeply sad piece—one that contrasts hugely with (in this case) an especially breezy finale sporting an irresistible and energetic main theme in "hunting" rhythm. Of course, it wouldn't be Bach without a few odd interruptions here and there, while the solo enters with a variation that really does show off his wonderfully improvisational compositional technique in a particularly clear way.

Wq 30 in B Minor (1753)

For this very large concerto Bach has arranged an opening that truly suggests the orchestra "speaking." It has a conversational character all by itself, and this virtually guarantees that the solo will have plenty of opportunity to engage the orchestra in close dialogue. Although the atmosphere is quite moody, there is a powerful undercurrent moving the music forward. The actual tempo is Allegro assai (very fast), but the broad phrasing disguises the actual speed and encourages a certain degree of rhetorical emphasis that spills over into the technically major-key Adagio. This is a deeply pathetic movement with lovely sustained harmonies over repeated bass notes. It's extremely affecting and emotionally satisfying. The finale is violent, strongly accented, and features some virtuoso fiddling for the orchestral violins, never mind the taxing solo part. The contrast between the two in the ensuing dialogue between them couldn't be greater. This is a concerto very rich in personality and in its depth of feeling.

Wq 31 in C Minor (1753)

There are a lot of ideas in the very long ritornello that opens this concerto, and in addition, the solo has independent material of its own. The movement has a somewhat combative character, with the two protagonists constantly interrupting each other. For example, the solo actually completes the ritornello, and then takes off on its own. The Adagio has the character of a nocturne: muted strings, very hushed, with a solemn tone and an open ending that leads straight to the very remarkable finale. Bach asks that the strings stay muted. The tempo is moderate—allegretto—and the character is subdued, as if the participants don't want to wake up after that haunting Adagio. Although the mutes come off at the very end, for a vigorous conclusion in dotted rhythms, it's clear that the emotional progression of the music has wholly determined the form.

Wq 32 in G Minor (1754)

Bach was on a roll with concertos in minor keys during this period, but when it comes to Wq 30–32, each is quite different in character. For this Concerto in G Minor, the opening Allegretto is serious, deliberate and thoughtful—although that doesn't mean boring. The first movement's dialogue is very rich in detail, while the moderate pace allows the listener time to take it all in. This concerto is not, in any event, one of the particularly lengthy ones. The slow movement adds flutes for extra color, and its calm melody contains some gentle dissonances to spice up the harmony. For the finale Bach offers a harsh, even grim minuet, a sort of "anti-galant" style that makes the music even more unsettling.

Wq 33 in F Major (1755)

This is one of those concertos easy to overlook, surrounded as it is by so many unambiguously great works, but it's a very worthwhile piece that breaks some new ground. The opening Allegretto is full of color and contrast, not just in theme but also in tempo, with the tension steadily building toward the end. Beginning in a galant style, the movement ends somewhere else entirely. The Adagio, too, is unexpected. It remains in a major key, and features a very beautiful, romantic melody in long, flowing phrases. After this heavenly interlude, the finale is extremely vigorous, even wild, and brings the work to a bracing conclusion.

Wq 34 in G Major (1755)

The opening ritornello is classic C. P. E.: sudden echoes, alternating major and minor, even and dotted rhythms—in short, maximum contrast. Believe it or not, this concerto may have been written originally for organ, and there's a version for flute, too (Wq 169). All three versions have been recorded, and the wonderfully witty pause in the opening solo sounds especially jolly on the organ—sort of like a carnival calliope. The slow movement is a very emotional, minor-key Largo with a long melody articulated in big phrases. A trill introduces the solo, seamlessly continuing the orchestral tune. The presto finale is full of bluster and high spirits, and the general shape of this concerto is very classical: a long first movement with a much lighter finale half the length.

Wq 35 in E-flat Major (1759)

This is the second concerto allegedly destined for the organ. It's a very compact work, less than twenty minutes long. As if to compensate for its brevity, the orchestra and the soloist enjoy a relaxed, conversational relationship, with the solo given its own brief introduction before the two share in a discussion of the ritornello. The slow movement, once again, remains in a major key, although the orchestral sonority is dark and Bach adds affecting dissonances to the melodic line. Marked "Adagio sostenuto," emotionally speaking this is very sophisticated music that repays close attention. The very quick finale continues the conversational dialogue between the solo and orchestra, with a few rhythmic tricks along the way to keep things interesting.

Wq 36 in B-flat Major (1762)

As you can see, Bach's output of concertos is beginning to slow down. Still in Berlin, he already had a very good stock of major works, and consequently less need to produce new ones. This concerto opens with a very short ritornello, relaxed in tempo, but very detailed in rhythm and harmony with its major key seemingly under constant threat. As in the previous concerto, the interaction between the solo and orchestra is courtly and gracious, but there's still an unusual degree of harmonic tension thanks to "wrong notes" in the melodic line. Also like the previous concerto, the slow movement, marked "Poco adagio," sticks with a major key, but Bach constantly varies the harmony, as he does in the triple-time finale. The three movements of this concerto seem all of a piece—an ongoing conversation exploring similar subjects from different perspectives.

Wq 37 in C Minor (1762)

The opening ritornello, with horns added to the orchestra, is heavy and doom-laden. It's a march, with breakaway fast passages, ending very abruptly. The solo takes up the ritornello right away and a tense dialogue evolves with the orchestra, based on bits of the theme. Marked "Andante ed arioso," the slow movement has a short introduction but no actual ritornello. It's a genuine song shared between the solo and the ensemble. For the finale, a Presto in 6/8 hunting meter, the two protagonists divide up the theme between them, often unpredictably, so you never really know who will get what.

Wq 38 in F Major (1763)

This very enjoyable concerto starts with a rollicking, good-humored ritornello. Listen to the left hand at the first entrance of solo. It offers a particularly good way to hear Bach's natural thinking in two parts—an expressive bass line with elaborate melodic figuration on top. In these later concertos, he is steadily loosening up the relatively strict alternation between solo and tutti sections of a typical movement in ritornello form. Instead, the solo and the orchestra are becoming increasingly integrated in continuous dialogue, a process very evident here. The minor-key Poco adagio features a very touching melody, with flutes doubling the strings. Perhaps its pathos has an impact on the harmonically very curious opening of finale, which only gradually works its way to a sunny, F major conclusion.

Wq 39 in B-flat Major (1765)

Well, it had to happen. I find this concerto to be boring, at least as originally composed for solo oboe. The opening Allegretto is very galant, but to my mind not in a good way, while the best part is certainly the very sad but lyrical Largo e mesto slow movement. The allegro moderato finale is pleasant, with gentle digressions and syncopations adding interest, but in general the piece suffers from a surfeit of moderate-to-slow music, an issue alleviated somewhat in the keyboard version with its perkier sonority and greater possibilities for virtuoso figuration. Also, the timbre of the oboe can be very fatiguing to the ear in large doses;

this just comes with the territory, and it takes a very great virtuoso with an uncharacteristically gorgeous tone to get around the problem (apologies to oboists everywhere). Let's face it, even geniuses have off days.

Wq 40 in E-flat Major (1765)

If you want to hear a great oboe concerto by Bach, this is just the ticket. He's back on form right from the syncopated opening, which seems relaxed but is actually full of latent energy. The phrasing is broad and lyrical, knit together by the presence of the opening rhythm. Full of passion and pathos, the minor-key Adagio ma non troppo is the longest movement, with a wonderfully sustained melodic line that's almost eerie at times. The solo emerges from the orchestral texture and then alternates freely with the larger ensemble, ignoring formal boundaries. Another surprise awaits us in the finale. It's a minuet, graceful, but unusually for the finale of a major-key work, it adopts a minor key until the end. This is, clearly, the natural emotional reaction to the intensity of the central adagio, and it produces a work of striking and unusual expressive depth, especially for an oboe concerto.

The Hamburg Concertos

Bach's situation in Hamburg, a large commercial metropolis and "free" city, was quite different from that in Berlin. As municipal director of music, he served an audience both larger and less musically sophisticated than his Berlin circle of friends and admirers. This is usually the excuse for arguing that his Hamburg works represent a dumbing-down of his music's bolder, more experimental tendencies. Certainly some of Bach's own statements and public advertisements suggest as much, but actual listening to the music tells a different story. In particular, rather than focusing on the "ridiculous specifications" that Bach mentions in connection with composing on commission, I would suggest that we give particular credence to his statement, "It may be that such unpleasant circumstances have challenged my genius to *certain inventions I might not otherwise have happened upon.*" For these are certainly what we hear in his last eleven concertos.

Wq 41 in E-flat Major (1769)

This is a very innovative, richly scored piece, with two flutes, two horns, and divided violas in the orchestra. The first movement alternates two tempos: an introductory Largo and the prestissimo main body of the movement. The Largo later returns in full, replacing the second appearance of the ritornello. There's also some very characterful writing for the solo, with added flutes and pizzicato strings. The result is music that mixes brilliance with ethereal sweetness, and provides for constant surprise. Remaining in the major, the delicious slow movement also features flutes with pizzicato strings and divided violas. It has an open ending leading directly to the finale, a lighthearted minuet marked in German "*Ziemlich geschwinde*" (moderately quick), sporting some especially witty and piquant writing for the solo.

Wq 42 in F Major (1770)

Composing in F major, Bach is often cheerful and uncomplicated. That is certainly true of this big-gestured ritornello, with its broad phrases that allow for lots of busy figuration from the solo (when it enters) under a steady chugging rhythm. The Larghetto again remains in a major key—you will note that this is becoming a trend—and the music reveals a touching innocence, leavened with a smidgeon of panic thanks to some rude accents and broken phrases. Marked "Poco presto," the finale is a hearty dance with a surprisingly sudden interruption in the ritornello. The keyboard and orchestra share the same material for most of this very good-natured, satisfying movement.

Six Keyboard Concertos, Wq 43 (1772)

No. 1 in F Major
No. 2 in D Major
No. 3 in E-flat Major
No. 4 in C Minor
No. 5 in G Major
No. 6 in C Major

This set of six concertos constitutes Bach's first major publication in Hamburg. Too much has been made of their supposed suitability for amateurs. While all six concertos are short (twelve to twenty minutes), the keyboard writing does not lack virtuoso elements, and it seems that this statement reflects, first, Bach's desire to maximize sales, and second, his putting all of the musical lines into the keyboard parts so as to make the works playable as solos, without the orchestra. That said, the orchestration, which includes flutes and horns, is lovely and very much to be desired. More important, formally speaking, these works show Bach at his most inventive and formally free. Every one of them does something remarkable and new.

For starters, all of the concertos are designed to be played continuously, without pauses between the movements. No. 3 comes closest to normalcy in this respect, in that the music does actually stop, but only after singularly interesting transitions leading us on to the next movement. Moreover, the thematic material of the larghetto slow movement slowly morphs into music from the first movement. No. 2 has two remarkable andante "interruptions" in the otherwise quick first movement, and this music, varied, reappears in the solo in the slow movement while the orchestra has different material. In No. 5, by contrast, the adagio introduction to the quick first movement returns in both the solo and the ensemble as the actual slow movement. Concerto No. 4 has four movements, the third of which is a minuet. But get this: the last movement is actually a continuation of the first, with the two central movements functioning as "interruptions." Bach refers to their main themes just before the end.

In short, Wq 43 is a sort of encyclopedia of all of the ways Bach can think of to create novel large forms in concerto style, and this discussion of form doesn't even begin to cover the expressive depth and variety that he builds into each piece. The presto finale of No. 3, for example, is particularly humorous, with a main theme that begins in the wrong key. No. 4's C minor pathos, however, has made it the most popular of the set. You'd have to be crazy to suggest that Bach found the circumstances of producing music for the wider Hamburg public in any way inhibiting. There are, incidentally, fine recordings available of all of these concertos, both individually and as a complete set.

Wq 44 in G Major (1778)

This short and charming concerto, only fifteen minutes long, continues the innovations characteristic of Wq 43. The first movement employs the standard ritornello from, but the minor-key Larghetto features a very brief orchestral opening continued immediately by the solo. By the time we get to the finale, the solo actually leads off, with a witty theme in short phrases that permit both keyboard and ensemble to indulge in plenty of humorous byplay. We are very, very close here to a recognizably "classical" style.

Wq 45 in D Major (1778)

As previously, the first movement is very clear formally, although the ritornello is quite short and the reminder of the movement features the solo and orchestra in close dialogue. The Andantino, in the minor, barely gets started before the solo enters, and shares its touchingly sad cantilena with the strings. This movement has both depth and great delicacy. The allegro finale is quite short, and very funny. The solo interrupts the last note of the ritornello, each time with something different. In these late concertos you may notice that the melodic material has become more tuneful, the phrasing less angular, but by no means square or insipidly "galant."

Wq 46 in F Major for Two Harpsichords and Orchestra (1740)

This concerto for two harpsichords has received a number of modern recordings, especially as a companion to some of J. S. Bach's double keyboard concertos. As with so much of C. P. E.'s music in F major, this piece is a high-spirited romp, at least in its outer movements. The scoring includes horns—raucous ones in most period instrument performances—and the opening ritornello includes a funny rhythmic hiccup that somehow always sounds fresh, no matter how many times you hear it. The solos have new material initially, but then Bach luxuriates in the many opportunities the medium affords for dialogue in differing textural combinations. Some of the rhythmic effects he produces are quite titillating. The minor-key Largo is a poignant nocturne, with affecting dissonances in the melodic line, while the finale is a virtuoso extravaganza that makes quite a racket once it gets going.

Wq 47 in E-flat Major for Harpsichord, Fortepiano, and Orchestra (1788)

Bach's last orchestral work, composed in the year of his death, was written for Sarah Levy (née Itzig) the daughter of a very wealthy Berlin Jewish family, and Felix Mendelssohn's great-aunt. She also commissioned Bach's three late quartets (Wq 93–95). Levy presided over a salon consisting of the cream of Berlin society. She was also a piano virtuoso, and most importantly, a major Bach collector. W. F. Bach was her piano teacher and friend (he composed a song for her wedding), and it is thanks to her and her extended family that many works of the Bach family survived. Their music collection was absorbed into the library of the Berlin Sing-Akademie; it is this archive that, when rediscovered in Kiev only in 1999, generated renewed interest in C. P. E. Bach and made publication of the new Complete Works possible.

It had been ten years since Bach had last written a concerto, but his imagination had not declined a bit. The scoring of this work, for harpsichord and fortepiano, is absolutely unique until the twentieth century, and the musical invention is of the highest quality throughout. Its humor is truly classical, from the witty opening ritornello to the boisterous interplay between the two soloists. The major-key Larghetto is graciously lyrical, its surface ruffled now and then by deep notes in the bass. The fragmentation of phrases between the two keyboards, violins, and flutes is delicious. The final Presto presents us with one of Bach's catchiest tunes. When played by the strings alone it may sound repetitious, but as distributed among all of the participants it becomes hilarious. This work is one of the most original and enjoyable concertos of the eighteenth century. It reveals Bach as a tireless champion of the new, and an innovator right until the very end.

4 Sonatinas for Keyboard(s) and Orchestra (1762–64)

Just what is a "sonatina" for keyboard and orchestra? The answer is that it's whatever Bach says it is, since no one before or since has ever written one. As a musical term, the word simply means "little sonata," and Bach wrote a delightful batch of them for keyboard (Wq 64) in the 1730s. Those, however, really are normal, three-movement pieces, some of which are longer than works given the standard "sonata" designation. He also wrote a few more single movements of very different character as teaching pieces to accompany his *Essay*. The music under consideration in this chapter, however, is quite different. The orchestral sonatinas have no generally consistent form, and several include arrangements of preexisting pieces, some of which get juxtaposed to create new and interesting larger structures.

All we know about these works is that in the years 1762–64, Bach took some time off from composing formal concertos, which are in fact sonatas for keyboard and orchestra, so as to turn out a dozen of these gems. During this period he wrote only a single concerto, Wq 38, in 1763, but otherwise produced nothing new in the genre until the oboe/harpsichord Concerto in B-flat of 1765. Three of the sonatinas (Wq 106–108) were published in earlier versions; below I list only the final revisions to avoid unnecessary duplication. The differences generally concern the difficulty of the solo writing, which Bach increased later on, turning what had been a peculiar form of hybrid orchestral work with prominent keyboard parts into a quasi-concerto.

Actually, these "little sonatas" aren't all that small. Despite the fact that some have only two movements, several are as big as full-fledged concertos, and the scoring is as colorful as any of the more lavishly endowed of Bach's more familiar concerted works—indeed, even more so. If the lack of symphonic development or emphasis on serious-sounding minor keys means that the music is lighter in tone than in some of his other efforts, the sonatinas are no less enjoyable for that. Only their uniqueness has prevented them from achieving the popularity that they deserve.

Six of the sonatinas include preexisting music, and six are entirely new. Where applicable I list the borrowings next to the relevant movement so that, if you are curious, you can compare the original pieces to these new incarnations.

Wq 96 in D Major

Scoring: Keyboard, Two Flutes, Two Horns, Two Violins, Viola, and Bass

1. *Andante ed arioso—Cembalo solo—Andante ed arioso—Cembalo solo—Andante ed arioso*
2. *Allegro*

Three of the sonatinas feature long, compound first movements in big alternating sections, rondolike. This one is particularly exquisite: first, the orchestra and soloist spin out a lovely movement in moderate tempo and vocal style. This is interrupted by the solo alone, after which the aria continues, leading to another solo in quicker tempo, and closing with the concluding portion of the aria. It's very difficult to describe the music's ear-catching charm and eloquence, but the piece is quite unforgettable once you hear it. Bach then wraps up the sonatina with a brief (only a bit more than two minutes), exuberant Allegro full of colorful interplay between the solo and the orchestra, especially the flutes.

Wq 97 in G Major

Scoring: Keyboard, Two Flutes, Two Horns, Two Violins, Viola, and Bass

1. *Andantino—Presto—Andantino—Presto—Andantino (Wq 81/11 and 81/4)*
2. *Tempo di Minuetto (Wq 81/1)*

Bach's set of Twelve Little Pieces, Wq 81, for two flutes (or violins) and keyboard served as the basis for this sonatina. In the first movement, two pieces, one slow, the other quick, alternate, rondo style, with varied keyboard figuration on the repeats. The second movement is a minuet alternating with entertaining and differently characterized keyboard solos, the second of which is very extensive and forms a complete piece all by itself. In other words, this sonatina's second movement follows the same formal plan as its first part: five sections linked in a chain, in this case comprising Minuet—Solo—Minuet—Solo—Minuet.

Incidentally, in case you're curious, there is no standardized spelling of *minuet* during this period. Bach used several different ones, perhaps depending on which language he was thinking in at any given time, or maybe based on the weather that day. It's a very random thing that we don't need to worry about.

Wq 98 in G Major

Scoring: Keyboard, Two Flutes, Two Horns, Two Violins, Viola, and Bass

1. *Larghetto*
2. *Allegro*
3. *Alla Polacca (Wq 117/22* L'Auguste*)*

The formal shape of slow—quick—quick (dance) appears in many of Bach's chamber works, and highlights a certain intimacy quite evident in the orchestral writing in many of these sonatinas. Note, for example, the particularly delightful interplay between the keyboard and the flutes in the opening Larghetto. The largest movement is the central Allegro, but even so the entire sonatina plays for less than ten minutes. For the finale Bach has chosen *L'Auguste*, a character piece in the form of a polonaise. As popular a dance in Bach's day as it remained throughout the nineteenth century (Bach's brother W. F. wrote a dozen of them for keyboard), the tempo of the polonaise is similar to that of the minuet, but the accent patterns are different and the rhythm more strongly marked, as you can hear in this example.

Wq 99 in F Major

Scoring: Keyboard, Two Flutes, Two Horns, Two Violins, Viola, and Bass

1. *Largo*
2. *Allegro*
3. *Andante*

Given the movement designations, you might think that the form of this piece would be basically the same as that of its predecessor, but you'd be wrong. The central allegro is very brief, with some deliciously tipsy writing for the soloist, while the finale is a rondo similar in shape to the first movement of Wq 96. The "ritornello," such as it is, has no parallel elsewhere in Bach's music. It consists of delicate flute solos alternating with furious orchestral outbursts. It comes to a full close. There are two episodes, both solos for the keyboard, the first in an affecting minor key. This throws the weight of the entire piece onto the finale, which is as long as the first two movements combined.

Wq 100 in E Major

Scoring: Keyboard, Two Flutes, Two Horns, Two Violins, Viola, and Bass
1. *Allegretto (Wq 117/29* La Xénophon/La Sybille*)*
2. *Allegretto (Wq 117/38* La Frédérique *and Wq 65/29/iii)*

The first movement of this sonatina consists of two of Bach's keyboard character pieces arranged in ABA form, with *La Xénophon* (student of Socrates and a Greek historian/scholar) a graceful movement in the major, and *La Sybille* a quicker piece in a contrasting minor key. The two works are paired in Bach's original conception as well, and designed to be played together exactly as he arranges them here. In the sonatina's second movement, also marked "Allegretto," the juxtaposition is even more interesting. Both *La Frédérique* and the finale of the Piano Sonata in E Major, Wq 65/29, are versions of the same piece, and this arrangement draws freely from them both. The music in all three versions is a triple-time dance very close in feeling to a minuet.

Wq 101 in C Major

Scoring: Keyboard, Two Flutes, Two Horns, Two Violins, Viola, and Bass
1. *Larghetto*
2. *Allegro*
3. *Alla polacca*

Although this slow-quick-dance tempo sequence might strike modern ears as unusual, this particular example turns out to be a remarkably well-balanced piece, with three movements of roughly equal length. The initial Larghetto is soothing, but the keyboard writing has just enough dissonance to add a touch of spice to the melodic line. After a very short couple of bars, the central Allegro features the orchestra and soloist in rapid dialogue throughout. The concluding polonaise has an appealingly rustic quality, with some delightful touches of scoring for the flutes. I should also mention that the performance of this sonatina in Miklós Spányi's complete concerto edition for BIS records is one of the best recordings in that series (and it comes with the sensational Concerto in A Minor, Wq 26, and the finer of the two concertos originally for oboe, that in E-flat Major, Wq 40).

Wq 102 in D Major

Scoring: Keyboard, Two Flutes, Two Horns, Two Violins, Viola, and Bass

1. *Allegretto grazioso—Presto—Allegretto grazioso—Presto—Allegretto grazioso (Wq 117/28* La Complaisante *and Wq 81/7)*
2. *Allegretto (H 585/iii; Wq 74/iii and Wq 117/36* La Louise*)*

The first movement of this sonatina closely resembles that of Wq 97, and for its presto sections draws from the same collection of small pieces for flutes and keyboard, Wq 81. This contrasts with another keyboard character piece, a fairly long Allegretto grazioso that Bach called *La Complaisante.* Both are (naturally) varied on repetition. This chain of movements makes for a very substantial unit about fourteen minutes long. The finale is a minuet in all but name. You might think it odd that a piece less than three minutes long has such a complicated list of sources, but the reality is that all three of those cited here are different versions of the same music. H 585 is a trio sonata for two violins and continuo; the last movement of Wq 74 is the same arranged as a "trio" for violin and two hands of the keyboard (more on this in the chapter on chamber music); while *La Louise* gives the music a name and a setting for keyboard solo. It is a lively and very charming movement, so Bach's fondness for it isn't at all surprising.

Wq 103 in C Major

Scoring: Keyboard, Two Flutes, Two Horns, Two Violins, Viola, and Bass

1. Arioso—Andante—Arioso (Wq 117/34 La Philippine *and Wq 116/18)*

2. Allegro (Wq 62/20/iii)

The first movement, which lasts a total of around ten minutes, consists of the Andantino (here marked "Andante") in D Minor, Wq 116/18, for solo keyboard, framed by another of Bach's character pieces, *La Philippine,* in which the orchestra participates alongside the soloist in a songful and aptly named "Arioso." In the finale, Bach expands the conclusion of his Sonata in C Major, Wq 62/10, into a full-length concerto movement in his ripest mature style. He does this by adding extended solos for the keyboard, and in the process the length of piece doubles from less than five minutes to around ten. It's very interesting to listen to both the original and this "grown-up" version, comparing both the form and the content. Bach's father was a master at adapting the same music to different purposes, and in this case we see that the apple has not fallen far from the tree.

Wq 104 in F Major

Scoring: Keyboard, Two Flutes, Two Horns, Two Violins, Viola, and Bass

1. Adagio

2. Allegro, ma non troppo

3. Allegretto

All of the music in this sonatina seems to be original, and although the key is nominally F major, the opening Adagio wavers between the major and minor modes in a most affecting way. Its actual key signature is D minor, and so we don't hear an unambiguous major key until the second movement. The finale is yet another piece in the tempo and style of a minuet. All three movements of this work are very highly developed, similar to concerto or sonata movements, and the piece lasts around twenty minutes in performance. It is thus, like several of the other sonatinas, a full-length concert work.

Wq 105 in E-flat Major

Scoring: Keyboard, Two Flutes, Two Horns, Two Violins, Viola, and Bass

1. *Largo*
2. *Allegro di molto*
3. *Tempo di minuetto*

The soloist leads off from the very start, with the orchestra following on the keyboard's initial gesture. In keeping with the tone of these introductory slow movements generally, the mood is serene, the orchestra and soloist engaging in gentle dialogue, in this case with the flutes very active as well. The central Allegro di molto features those rapid exchanges between the solo and orchestra that are so much a feature of Bach's concerto style, while the final minuet provides a graceful and very harmonious conclusion.

Wq 109 in D Major

Scoring: Two Keyboards; Two Flutes, Two Oboes, Two Horns, Three Trumpets, Timpani, Two Violins, Viola, Cello, and Bassoon (Bass)

1. *Presto—Arioso—*Ein wenig lebhafter*—Presto—Arioso (Wq 117/37* La Gause*)*
2. *Tempo di minuetto—Allegro—Tempo di minuetto (Wq 117/18* La Pott*)*

This sonatina gets some play because it makes a logical coupling on disc with Bach's pair of concertos for two keyboards, Wq 46 and 47. The scoring is also very lavish, with trumpets, horns, oboes, and timpani making a glorious noise in louder passages. Bach's character piece *La Gause* comprises the Arioso sections of the first movement. The Prestos are militant fanfares for the full ensemble, while the central *Ein wenig lebhafter* (slightly livelier) features the two keyboards. Incidentally, there is no reason why the two soloists have to use identical instruments. Spányi on his BIS recording uses a harpsichord and a fortepiano, as Bach himself did in his later concerto, Wq 47. In the finale, the minuet that Bach called *La Pott* frames an eccentric Allegro for the keyboards, with rude interjections from the orchestra. It's all great fun.

Wq 110 in B-flat Major

Scoring: Two Keyboards, Two Flutes, Two Horns, Two Violins, Viola, and Bass
1. Andante
2. Allegro moderato (Wq 117/20 La Bergius*)*
3. Allegretto (Wq 62/16/iii)

Bach's final sonatina in this series, although scored for two keyboards, is a relatively intimate work. The first movement features a close dialogue between the orchestra and the soloists, with the horns participating from the start (unusual in what is technically a slow movement). Bach's character piece *La Bergius*—doubled in length to about four minutes through the simple expedient of varying the repeats and giving solo licks to the keyboards—forms the sonatina's winsome centerpiece, while the finale is an arrangement of the last movement of an actual sonata, Wq 62/16, also in B-flat major. Bach extends the movement in the same way as he does *La Bergius*, and as long as the two keyboards are well differentiated in timbre, there seems no limit to the range of colorful combinations at his disposal.

Bach did nothing without good reason, but the truth is that we have no clue regarding the specific occasions for which these works were written. They may fall into the category of music for popular public consumption, containing as they do "more sugar" than some of the concertos, but I always worry about making such assumptions. After all, we don't know what else appeared on the programs with them; and although this is undoubtedly "nice" music, with fewer shocking moments than we find in many of Bach's contemporaneous works in large forms, his imaginative variety and consistently inventive approach to structure reveal the same thoughtfulness that stamps just about everything that he wrote. There's a lot going on in these sonatinas, and especially in those works that incorporate preexisting music we learn just how interesting some innocuous little pieces can be when placed cleverly, in the right context.

In closing this survey of the sonatinas, I want to take a moment to give a another shout-out to the indefatigable scholars at the Packard Humanities Institute whose contribution to the Complete Works has not only resurrected these pieces from an undeserved obscurity, it has identified the original sources of their many constituent parts. I have drawn on their work shamelessly in order to describe the music to you, and I can only express shock and awe at their achievement.

5 Bach's Eighteen Symphonies

These symphonies display precisely the novelty and originality that astonishes one so greatly in all Bach's works and make an indescribable effect when they are well performed by a suitable ensemble. Some time ago we heard them performed by an orchestra of some forty players, directed by the Herr Kapellmeister himself. Each symphony was played twice, and we will never forget the impression that this music made on us. . . .

—Anonymous Hamburg critic in 1780, describing the four Orchestral Symphonies with Twelve Obbligato Parts[12]

C. P. E. Bach's eighteen symphonies represent milestones in the evolution of the genre, as well as a series of very remarkable individual works. In order to understand why, we need to take a moment to consider just how counterintuitive the notion of a symphony really is. Nowadays we still regard a great symphony as the pinnacle of orchestral music, perhaps of instrumental composition more generally. This level of respect stems from the great works in the German tradition, beginning with Haydn. Before that, in the 1740s and '50s, the symphony as an independent concert piece, with roots in the Italian *sinfonia*, was best described by its alternative eighteenth-century designation: overture. In other words, it was a light, generally brief curtain-raiser to the main event. It didn't really matter whether this was an opera, a play, or the remainder of a concert featuring big-name soloists, whether instrumental or vocal.

Table 2: C. P. E. Bach Symphonies

Work	Wq	Year	Notes
Berlin Symphonies			
Symphony in G Major	173	1741	Keyboard Version Wq 122/1
Symphony in C Major	174	1755	
Symphony in F Major	175	1755	Keyboard Version Wq 122/2
Symphony in D Major	176	1755	
Symphony in E Minor	177	printed 1759	Version for strings of Wq 178
Symphony in E Minor	178	1756	Slow movement used in Sonata in G Minor Wq 62/18; Keyboard Version Wq 122/3
Symphony in E-flat Major	179	1757	
Symphony in G Major	180	1758	Keyboard Version Wq 112/13
Symphony in F Major	181	1762	Keyboard Version Wq 122/5
Six Symphonies for Baron van Swieten (Hamburg Symphonies)			
Symphony No. 1 in G Major	182/1	1773	For strings
Symphony No. 2 in B-flat Major	182/2	1773	For strings
Symphony No. 3 in C major	182/3	1773	For strings
Symphony No. 4 in A Major	182/4	1773	For strings
Symphony No. 5 in B Minor	182/5	1773	For strings
Symphony No. 6 in G Major	182/6	1773	For strings
Four Orchestral Symphonies with Twelve Obbligato Parts			
Symphony No. 1 in D Major	183/1	1776	2 fl, 2 ob, 1 bn, 2 hn, 5-part strings
Symphony No. 2 in E-flat Major	183/2	1776	2 fl, 2 ob, 1 bn, 2 hn, 5-part strings
Symphony No. 3 in F Major	183/3	1776	2 fl, 2 ob, 1 bn, 2 hn, 5-part strings
Symphony No. 4 in G Major	183/4	1776	2 fl, 2 ob, 1 bn, 2 hn, 5-part strings

Then, as now, it was famous individuals who drew the crowds and sold tickets, not works for ensemble. We talk about great presidents and prime ministers, not great parliaments and congresses. Credit for a major company's success (or blame for its failure) goes to its chairman or president, not to its secretaries and tradespeople. How strange it is, then, that we attach a singular value to a work written for an assemblage of largely nameless performers cooperating selflessly toward a shared goal. The only thing that made it possible was the fact that certain aristocrats in Vienna, or Mannheim, or Berlin spent a lot of money hiring large numbers of musicians, and insisted on getting the maximum bang for their buck.

Certainly there was no popular demand for music specifically designed for such a curious aggregate to play on its own. No one could have predicted the symphony's international success. That only came much later, in the 1790s, when Haydn proved that the symphony actually could become a featured concert event in Paris and London. He famously credited his isolation on Prince Esterházy's Hungarian estate for forcing him to become original in developing his symphonies, and had the prince not specifically asked for them, the history of music as we know it would have been very different.

Bach didn't have much opportunity to write symphonies, and the ones that have survived fall into three groups: the early works, Wq 173–81, written in Berlin between approximately 1741 and 1758; the six symphonies for strings, composed in 1773 on commission by Baron Gottfried van Swieten, Wq 182; and the four Orchestral Symphonies with Twelve Obbligato Parts of 1775, Wq 183—the only ones published in Bach's lifetime. As with so much of Bach's music, these symphonies have been underestimated, mostly because they are short (eight to twelve minutes on average), adopt the older three-movement, fast-slow-fast Italian *sinfonia* form, and because the concertos are so much larger and more numerous. For these reasons it may appear that Bach didn't give his symphonies much thought. Nothing could be further from the truth.

As the quotation at the head of this chapter makes clear, he definitely intended his symphonies to be feature events, and he played them that way in concert. They were, in this respect, far ahead of their time, and it is precisely because the symphony had not yet attained the status of "public spectacle" in the popular sense that Bach's turned out to be so special. There is very little evidence, either biographical or purely musical, that in writing them he felt compelled to make many artistic compromises—if that is what "popular" art usually entails. The six string symphonies of 1773 were specifically composed with the mandate from Baron van Swieten that Bach should feel free to do exactly as he pleased, and write without inhibition or regard for convention (not that he ever needed much encouragement in that direction).

Bach composed the four late symphonies for his own concerts in Hamburg, and however compact they turned out to be, they clearly were designed to showcase his imagination and daring. The fact that he had each work played twice on a single program to ensure comprehension points to the music's special qualities, as does the large ensemble assembled for the occasion. Even the earlier Berlin symphonies reveal the same love of contrast and surprise that we find in the best of the contemporary concertos. They're just shorter.

From the start then, Bach was a more serious, more ambitious, and perhaps more talented symphonist that just about any of his contemporaries, Haydn and Mozart aside, both of whom he largely predated. He may not have known where the medium was going, and he did not participate in its evolution in the same fashion as those later composers, but you cannot listen to his contributions to the literature without getting the sense that he understood its potential and was determined to put his own personal stamp as much on the symphony as on everything else that he touched.

One of the ways Bach did this was by asking that some or all of the movements of a symphony be played without a break. This might not seem like a big deal, and it happens in plenty of his other works too, but it's especially noticeable in the symphonies. This means that he had to give serious consideration to the question of how the various parts of a work relate to one another, and whether the transitions should be smooth, abrupt, or something in between. In other words, Bach had a tendency, particularly evident in these pieces, to see a work whole—to think of it as a single entity rather than as a series of more or less individual bits casually organized in related keys.

Remember, this was at a time when a concert might start with the first couple of movements of a symphony on the first half and conclude with the rest after intermission. Or favorite movements might be inserted into different works, as happened a couple of decades after Bach's death when the famous Allegretto of Beethoven's Seventh replaced the second movement of his Eighth. It would be inconceivable to treat these symphonies in such a cavalier fashion. You play them the way Bach wrote them, or you don't play them at all.

C. P. E.'s conception of the symphony remained relatively consistent throughout his career. First movements are often, but not always, the most important. They contain no sectional repeats, and are through-composed in a sort of modified ritornello form, which means that they can do just about anything. Their course is dictated by the expressive potential of their material. The central slow movements range from short transitional passages to lengthier pieces of great expressive depth. Many are cast in surprising keys that contrast boldly with the music on either side of them. The conclusions are usually dancelike movements or very quick finales in two halves, both repeated, which means that they can display a type of sonata form permitting some real symphonic development. For more on how this operates you can read my discussion of the Sonata in F Minor, Wq 57/6, in the chapter on the keyboard works.

By insisting on the unity and integrity of the individual work, Bach was doing something truly new, raising purely orchestral music to a higher level of sophistication and importance. The symphonies may be brief, especially when each movement is taken singly, but Bach's vision in composing them was notably large. They pack a big punch into a small space, and for that reason offer a great deal of listening satisfaction, both on initial acquaintance as well as on repetition. Some of them, notably the symphonies for Baron van Swieten, Wq 182, and the Symphony in D Major, Wq 183/1, have become relatively popular in recent decades both in concert and on recordings, especially with chamber orchestras and period instrument ensembles. With their formal originality and emotional richness, Bach's symphonies take their place proudly among the great works that justify our modern reverence for the medium.

Before discussing the works individually, let's take a detailed look at the piece included with this book: the Symphony in C Major, Wq 182/3, for string orchestra and continuo.

Symphony in C Major, Wq 182/3, for string orchestra and continuo

First Movement: Allegro assai

I mentioned that in the symphonies the first movements are usually the most important. Here is an exception to that rule, and there are others in Wq 182 as well. This opening movement lasts less than three frantic minutes. It begins memorably, with a leaping figure followed by a pause, and a trill. This gesture should be familiar if you have already read the chapter on the concertos. A short, distinctive motive followed by loud trill, often after a sudden pause, is one of C. P. E. Bach's personal fingerprints in quick music, and we also heard it in the Keyboard Concerto in D Minor, Wq 23—twice, in fact, in the first and last movements. In minor keys, it's an angry gesture like the roaring of a lion, but here, in a more amiable context, it comes across like a puppy shaking itself dry after a bath.

The rest of the movement contains two other main ideas: rushing violins with long notes in the bass, and a timid interlude in even rhythm. Bach varies and alternates this material with his usual freedom, interspersed with a couple of brief episodes, and the entire point of the music's bustling activity is that it could keep running around in circles forever unless something dramatic happens to change its course.

Second Movement: Adagio

That dramatic something is this Adagio, which follows without a break. The form is a simple ABABABA, in which "A" is a really shocking, loud dissonant scream incorporating the interval of a tritone—three whole steps, called "the devil in music" during the Middle Ages—followed by a softly sobbing figure, and "B" is a very sad but quite beautiful lament. As usual with Bach, each repeat of these ideas is subtly varied, and the music's emotional intensity makes this movement the true heart of the symphony. The harmonic and textural contrast with the initial Allegro is really jarring, which of course is Bach's clear intention. Although the Adagio comes to a full close, the last movement also follows immediately.

Third Movement: Allegretto

The finale brings soothing emotional relief in the form of a stately dance, still serious in tone but calmly purposeful in rhythm. Although in a theoretically "cheerful" major key, the music frequently detours into the minor, and features a closing theme based on a slithery, rising chromatic scale (that is, moving in half-steps) that's more than a little disturbing. This is also the longest and most fully developed part of the symphony, being composed in genuine sonata form: two halves, both repeated, the second of which incorporates a full development section based mostly on the movement's opening bars, and featuring some wonderful harmonic shifts. It rounds off the symphony in a satisfying way both emotionally and formally.

In reviewing samples for listening, I chose this symphony (as you may have guessed) because of the way its slow movement highlights the music's emotional extremes. It isn't atypical of Bach, but it does illustrate and allow you to hear with particular clarity his practice of thinking in terms of the entire sequence of feelings being presented. When you listen to the rest of Wq 182, think about how tellingly he has planned each movement so that the complete symphony adds up to an expressive whole. I stress this because it's very common in the literature to dwell on Bach's freakishness and seeming spontaneity, and let's face it, that's often the most fun—both to talk about and listen to—but it's also necessary to understand that there's a real guiding intelligence behind Bach's method, as well as a genuinely sympathetic personality. Both of these qualities seem to me especially evident here.

The Berlin Symphonies

Symphony in G Major, Wq 173

Scoring: Strings and Continuo

Bach's first symphony already shows evidence of the composer to come. The first movement, with its opening motive in syncopated rhythm, has that special energy and drive that quickly became his trademark, while the central Andante creates the impression of a slightly sinister march thanks to the constant underlying pulse. The concluding Allegretto is actually quicker than its heading might seem because the quick meter (3/8) and frequent recourse to sixteenth notes give the music something of the quality of a frantic minuet, interrupted by lyrical episodes and a few sudden outbursts. The melody itself is very memorable.

Symphony in C Major, Wq 174

Scoring: Two Flutes, Two Horns, Strings, and Continuo

The key of C major often brings out a particular boldness in Bach, and that's saying a lot. We heard that in Wq 182/3, just discussed, and you will also hear it in this first movement. Surprisingly, however, the music does not end in high spirits, but gently subsides into the gracious Andante, which stays in a major key, and drops the horns but retains the flutes (some recordings omit them, too). The bouncy finale, with its often repeated opening tune and only a couple very brief digressions into minor keys confirms this symphony as one of Bach's most cheerful orchestral pieces.

Symphony in F Major, Wq 175

Scoring: Two Flutes, (sometimes Two Bassoons), Two Horns, Strings, and Continuo

With the opening theme, we instantly know who the composer is: the leaping figuration, soft minor-key interruption, and surprising loud outburst all say "Bach" right from the start. The scoring also permits the horns and flutes a welcome degree of freedom and exposure. Although nominally in a minor key, the main theme of the Andante isn't at all dark or menacing; rather, it has a memorably exotic, almost Slavic quality that we will meet much later in many of Haydn's similarly memorable slow movements (think of Symphony No. 103). The flutes in unison with the violins add a beautifully cool touch of color that complements the tune perfectly. For the finale, Bach has another surprise in store: a "Tempo di menuetto" in rondo form, completely through composed (no formal repeats), with a very catchy ritornello and some lovely episodes in the minor.

Symphony in D Major, Wq 176

Scoring: Two Flutes, Two Horns, Three Trumpets, Two Horns, Timpani, Strings, and Continuo

The scoring of this symphony speaks volumes. This is the only one to use trumpets and timpani, and Bach deploys them with an almost fiendish relish. As in the previous symphonies, the slow movement leaves everyone out except the flutes and strings, but it also features two episodes for just the strings played pizzicato (plucked), a very surprising and colorful effect, especially in music of such charm. Bach has already figured out how to use his orchestra with imagination and flair. The finale features a "hunting" meter (6/8) guaranteed to bring the proceedings to a rousing conclusion. It's interesting to note that Bach adds a brief coda to the second half, thus justifying the repeat and offering yet more evidence that nothing in his music should be considered routine.

Symphony in E Minor, Wq 178

Scoring: Two Flutes, Two Oboes, Two Horns, Strings, and Continuo

"What happened to Wq 177?" you may well ask. Well, it's actually the strings only version of Wq 178. So, we don't need to worry about it at all. The first movement presents Bach in all of his familiar minor-key ferocity. The sinister opening, complete with a panicked initial outburst, shows the composer operating at full force. Bach also gives us a slow movement in perfect sonata form: AABA, with a repeated exposition and an absolutely regular recapitulation. The music's formal shapeliness and melodic grace represents the perfect foil to the turbulent opening, and in yet another striking the contrast the finale sounds quite eccentric, even humorous, despite its minor mode. An opening tune in dotted rhythms hops about like the plague of frogs in Handel's *Israel in Egypt*. This alternates with more evenly flowing, lyrical music. It's very distinctive, and as in the previous symphony the second half has a coda that concludes the argument, this time brusquely and emphatically.

Symphony in E-flat Major, Wq 179

Scoring: Two Oboes, Two Horns, Strings, and Continuo

This symphony takes off like a shot, prestissimo, which basically means as fast as possible, and the story this movement tells seems to be an effort to maintain that initial impetus no matter what diversions Bach places in its way. Eventually the racing strings quiet down and the music glides gently into the elegiac Larghetto, for strings and continuo alone. There are some very passionate moments in this brief four minutes of song that sound strikingly romantic—a vision of the future. The finale is another Presto in 6/8 hunting meter, and this one really emphasizes that "outdoors" quality thanks to the participation of the oboes and horns.

Symphony in G Major, Wq 180

Scoring: Two Oboes, Two Horns, Strings, and Continuo

Here we have another symphony that starts with great energy, Allegro di molto this time, but the expected quiet interruptions have a chirpy, humorous quality (due to the oboes) that points to music of a very different character than we often hear from Bach in aggressive mode. Nevertheless, the mood turns serious as the movement ends softly and inconclusively in the minor, setting up a slow movement that is very slow indeed—largo. It presents two characters in dialogue, much as we heard in the slow movement of the Keyboard Concerto, Wq 23: loud proclamations in dotted rhythm alternating with softer, more lyrical pleas. The finale is a march that wants to break out into a run, and often does.

Symphony in F Major, Wq 181

Scoring: Two Flutes, Two Oboes, Two Horns, Strings and Continuo

The opening movement is a riot: frantic triplets alternating with a melody in dotted rhythm that makes the piece sound sort of like a German classical version of the "Mexican Hat Dance." Bach's winding-down transition to the slow movement is particularly marvelous. Featuring flutes plus strings and continuo *tasto*, which means to just play the bass line without adding any harmonic filler, this soulful movement continues the music's dancelike rhythmic pulse. Indeed, the constant triplet rhythm of the opening movement combined with this 6/8 Andante and the 3/4 Finale, as well as the fact that all three movements get played without a break, results in music almost entirely in some version of triple time. It's very evidently all of a piece, and one of the breeziest works that Bach ever wrote.

If you take a look at the chart of the symphonies that accompanies this chapter (Table 2), you will see that four of these works also exist as transcriptions for solo keyboard. This was Bach's way to increase their exposure by giving listeners the opportunity to play the music at home or in more intimate surroundings. It's always interesting to hear arrangements like these if you have the time and inclination. The slow movement of the Symphony in E Minor also turns up in the Sonata in G Minor Wq 62/18. This is the group of twenty-four sonatas that were published during Bach's lifetime in miscellaneous collections. Sometimes the reuse of a movement points to the popularity of a particular piece, or the fact that it had special significance and value for the composer. Or it can just mean that he was running short of time and had to meet a deadline.

Hamburg Symphonies for Baron van Swieten, Wq 182

Scoring: Strings and Continuo

No. 1 in G Major

The first movements of all of these symphonies have a certain kaleidoscopic quality produced by using short, highly contrasted motives in a continuous play of texture and tempo. A movement such as this Allegro di molto technically retains that speed throughout, but by using alternately long and short note values Bach creates music that seems to move at different speeds. All the movements in this symphony are connected as well. The central Poco adagio stays for the most part in a major key, but it faces several alarming interruptions along the way to the swashbuckling presto finale. Four out of the six works in this group, including this one, feature finales that are the largest and most fully developed of the three movements—an innovation not generally seen again in the symphonic world until much later.

No. 2 in B-flat Major

The opening movement, while beginning with Bach's customary energy, has a more pensive and lyrical character than its predecessor, partly the result of more quiet music. The slow movement, again remaining in the major, leaves out the continuo keyboard entirely, and features some delicate pizzicato commentary from the cellos and basses that's quite touching. Its melodic ideas have an especially lovely, wistful quality, but the movement is very short and the racy and the substantial finale, marked "presto," blows it away with a shocking interruption after which the music never looks back. Bach adds a brief but very satisfying coda to the second half repeat. Here is clearly a symphony in which everything points to the finale.

No. 3 in C Major

This symphony is included with the samples for listening and covered in detail above.

No. 4 in A Major

The weight of this symphony rests with the first movement, and it contains an amazing richness of ideas within a very short space. There are four in the first few seconds alone: a sort of etude for the violins, a strong unison statement for the full ensemble, a soft lyrical phrase, and lastly a longer, vigorous outburst. Although the form is basically the same as in the previous works, the music has a more vigorous "developmental" feel that confirms the movement's importance. The modulation to the central Largo ed innocentemente is just wonderful: it sounds as though Bach is picking up the movement somewhere in the middle, and once again the music has a romantic quality that sounds absolutely timeless. It's so beautiful that the start of the finale comes as a shock, and it takes some time before we recover. This is, however, also a very substantial finale—indeed, this is the longest symphony of the set, about twelve minutes in all.

No. 5 in B Minor

This is the only other symphony by Bach after Wq 178 to be set in a minor key, and it's a particularly affecting piece. The opening movement is unique in that it moves at a moderate allegretto tempo. It features three different kinds of music: an opening march, rapid exchanges between the various string sections, and a sad, pleading melody high in the violins. The movement is very incomplete; as with the Fourth Symphony in this group Bach runs smack into the slow movement, and picks it up in midstride. A brief piece, it spends most of its two and three-quarter minutes remaining in or around minor keys. The finale, too, begins as if already in progress. It contains several memorable ideas, including an intense passage in long notes, fortissimo, that isn't really a "theme" at all as much as an angry gesture. For the second-half repeat, Bach has composed his longest coda yet.

No. 6 in E Major

The opening movement has a sunny quality and a vital rhythmic swing produced by its being in 3/4 time—quick waltz tempo, in fact—and the principal idea really sings. Had it been just a bit longer you might mistake it for a lost Viennese classic, and the melodic catchiness characterizes the entire symphony. It's amazing how many different ways in these works Bach finds to surprise us with the start of the slow movement. The music makes as if to end boldly, except the final note to complete the cadence is missing. Instead, there's a pause, and the Poco andante begins, seemingly in the minor, but only momentarily before the serene principal theme sails in. Although this movement comes to a definite conclusion, it's only so that Bach can launch the next one as if already in progress. We are now back among the symphonies whose weight falls on the finale. A bit like that of the E minor Symphony, this conclusion features lots of music in dotted rhythms, only with a greater degree of muscularity, even roughness. It brings the entire set of six to a singularly gutsy and emphatic close.

Four Orchestral Symphonies with Twelve Obbligato Parts, Wq 183

Scoring: Two Flutes, Two Oboes, Bassoon, Two Horns, Strings, and Continuo (5 parts)

No. 1 in D Major (Wq 183/1)

Obbligato simply means "obligatory" in the sense that the parts are necessary, not optional, and also sometimes that they should be played strictly as written. With these symphonies Bach discovered the joys of orchestral color, using his diverse ensemble for maximum contrast and variety. The D Major Symphony has stood as the watchword for all that Bach was about as a symphonist. Its opening is incredibly arresting—music of astonishing excitement and tension that keeps building in one of the great orchestral pile-ups in eighteenth-century music. The first movement is simply one of the wildest pieces that Bach, or anyone else, ever wrote, and yet it ends gently, as we have come to expect, making a transition to the Largo.

This tiny movement, barely two minutes long, is exquisitely scored for two flutes, pizzicato violins, solo viola and cello, basses, and no harpsichord. Despite his comments to the contrary, Bach was evidently well aware that the continuo wasn't quite as necessary as he had asserted a couple of decades previously in his *Essay*. The concluding Presto has a rollicking rhythm that stops dead on several occasions for a mysterious interlude with strangely disquieting harmonies. There is a substantial coda added to the second half repeat. In short, it's vintage C. P. E.

No. 2 in E-flat Major (Wq 183/2)

Whereas the opening of Symphony No. 1 in this set built (and built, and built) to an overwhelming climax, this symphony starts off at full tilt. The opening group of ideas features one that's truly grotesque: a sequence of loud trills. Remember the image of that puppy shaking itself dry? Bach also has a good time contrasting the bluster of the full orchestra to a timid solo for the first flute player. This movement, crazy trills and all, flows right into the Larghetto, which begins with one of those magical chords that instantly transport us elsewhere. The main idea, though, is another flute solo, alerting us to the fact that Bach understands that timbre alone can be a unifying principle in larger structures. As in the previous symphony, this slow movement is very short, really little more than a connecting link to the finale, another of those Allegrettos that seems to go much more quickly than you'd think because of the small note values and rapid passagework for the violins. No coda this time, though: the end of the second half repeat really is the end. Period.

No. 3 in F Major (Wq 183/4)

This symphony begins with another impressive crescendo of power and tension, and like that at the start of the D Major Symphony, this one leads to a passage for solo woodwinds, only here the quick figurations persist throughout, maintaining the initial tempo. The transition to the slow movement is very extensive in this piece, and the Larghetto, when it finally arrives, turns out to be scored initially for the viola and cello sections alone—a very eccentric choice. Bach marks the lines "tutti," meaning that everyone plays, and also that he probably expected to have an orchestra on hand of some size, and not the usual pint-size period instrument band that we often hear on recordings. Once again the keyboard is silent, the mood solemn and austere.

Although by no means long, this slow movement is longer than the previous two, and it comes to a definite conclusion. However Bach still directs that the finale should follow without pause. It's a beefy, athletic movement with some particularly bold writing for the horns, and once again it has no need of a coda.

No. 4 in G Major (Wq 183/4)

This first movement gets going at full bore right from the start. The initial idea, with its three repeated notes at the beginning of each phrase, undergoes a good bit of transformative development and is very easy to hear whenever it occurs (repeated notes are particularly good for that). The second movement, scored for strings and flutes, at nearly five minutes turns out to be the most fully developed slow piece in any of these symphonies. It has two halves, both repeated, plus an extensive coda. The music moves with a stately grace, often in dotted rhythms. The mood is sad but stoic, not sentimental. For the finale, Bach returns to his favorite 6/8 hunting rhythm, with the horns well to the fore. It's an ebullient conclusion that features a motive with three strong chords—featuring rising rather than repeated notes—that still can't help but remind us of the symphony's very beginning. The sectional endings aren't bold enough to make an effective conclusion; Bach evidently agrees and so provides a rambunctious coda.

You may notice that there are no sanctioned keyboard transcriptions of Wq 182 and 183. Of course, there could be any number of reasons for this, but I believe the explanation stems from the fact that the music is so intimately wound up with the sound of the orchestra that Bach could not reimagine it in other terms. This is particularly true of these last four symphonies, marvelous examples of music by a genuinely symphonic thinker, even though circumstances dictated that he devote more of his time and effort to other media.

6 A Vocal Interlude

Your Honor is completely correct when you say that devout feelings are precisely those which are expressed most properly in music, and I, as a clavier player, dare to claim that one can actually say a great deal on our instrument with a good performance. I exclude here the mere tickling of the ears and demand that the heart should be moved. Such a clavier player, especially if he has a highly inventive genius, can do a great deal. However, words always remain words and the human voice always has an advantage over us.

—C. P. E. Bach letter to Heinrich Wilhelm von Gerstenberg, 21 October 1771[13]

Do not linger here, imitator,
For you must blush with shame if you remain.
Carl Philipp Emanuel Bach,
The most profound harmonist,
United originality with beauty,
Was great
When accompanying the word,
But still greater
In bold wordless music:
Surpassing the inventor of keyboard instruments.

—From Friedrich Klopstock's epitaph for C. P. E. Bach[14]

Dealing with C. P. E. Bach's vocal music is a tricky proposition. Because his modern reputation depends almost exclusively on his instrumental pieces, you might think that he lavished far less effort on the medium, but the reality is far more complex. What is true, however, is that Bach's engagement with music for the voice was even more contingent on his personal and professional circumstances than was his instrumental output. During his lifetime, it may surprise you to learn that some of his most popular and widely circulated compositions were songs. Bach wrote several hundred of them, most set to German sacred poetry. They were just the sort of thing designed to appeal to the religious values of eighteenth-century, middle-class North German music consumers, and consequently hardly a product that would attract much attention today. We will consider them briefly for the sake of completeness, but I am the last person to suggest that you make them a listening priority however lovely some of them undoubtedly are.

As a composer of larger sacred and secular works, Bach's opportunities were limited. Unlike his younger brother Johann Christian, he was not interested in opera, and particularly not the Italian style of comic opera that became prevalent in his day. Bach regarded that as we might view trash TV. During his time in Berlin working for Frederick the Great he was not asked and never tried to contribute to the repertoire of works in the old, baroque *opera seria* style—a good thing, as it turned out given Frederick's rigidly stale tastes—nor did he have much chance to write sacred music. The king was, at best, a deist (remember that his BMF [best male friend] was Voltaire) who loathed organized religion, and Bach's job never gave him the opportunity to write for the Berlin churches. His single major sacred work from the Berlin years, the Magnificat, is a masterpiece, but it remained an isolated one.

After 1868, in Hamburg, Bach was indeed in charge of sacred music for the municipal churches, and he arranged a lot of it. I say "arranged" deliberately. His major efforts include more than twenty Passion settings assembled largely from pieces by earlier composers: his father, his godfather Telemann, and contemporary sacred music specialists, such as Gottfried Homilius (1714–85). Bach only contributed as much original music as he deemed necessary to set the text, and even if we wanted to listen to these pieces, we had no opportunity until after they were rediscovered in Kiev and returned to Germany in 2001. The three big sacred oratorios on the other hand—*Die Israeliten in der Wüste* (The Israelites in the Desert), *Die Auferstehung und Himmelfahrt Jesu* (The Resurrection and Assumption of Jesus), and *Passions-Cantate* (The Passion Cantata)—are major works, popular in their day, expressive, beautifully written, and certainly palatable to modern audiences, but still not exactly "greatest hits" material.

Bach also wrote and/or arranged a great deal of ceremonial music for the installation of Hamburg clergyman and city officials. Again much of it was considered lost until very recently, and it is only just now (2015) being published. Any assessment of how effective these works are will have to await the accumulation of at least a minimal performance history, as well as the sorting out of the provenance of all of the music that they contain. The circumstances of these commissions don't look terribly promising, however thrilling an occasion the arrival of a new minister for one of the major churches might have been. The fact is that German Protestant sacred music at this time was suffering a period of decline, for reasons to be considered shortly. City officials also were notoriously tight-fisted, and as a result, despite Bach's efforts, performance standards were iffy at best. Bach's oratorios and his best original sacred pieces (the *Heilig* for two orchestras and choirs, for example) appeared in his own public concerts, and not just in the churches.

If the foregoing summarizes why Bach's output for voice assumed the form it did, we must still heed the distinction between music for voices and music written in the vocal style. As we have already seen from Bach's own words, making keyboard instruments "sing" was pretty much his life's ambition. It was expected that the best instrumental music aspired to vocal expressivity and a specificity of meaning similar to that communicated through the use of words, and Bach's was praised precisely for these qualities. Nevertheless, then as now, vocal music was the most popular because it was the most readily understood, and for that reason alone it enjoyed the greatest chance of survival over time. Great singers received the highest fees and attracted the largest crowds. Bach's own concerts were liberally peppered with vocal works, as were most such events, and it was in this very period that the choral masterpieces of Handel started to become the foundation of what we now call "classical music."

Bach was well aware that a composer's posthumous reputation likely would rest on works written for the voice, even though it was not his particular specialty. He could see it happening in his own time with such pieces as Handel's *Messiah*, which he programmed in Hamburg, and from the huge ongoing popularity of Carl Heinrich Graun's 1755 oratorio *Der Tod Jesu* (The Death of Jesus), one of the models for his own oratorios. You might think that Passion music, such as Graun's, would hardly be popular at any time except on Good Friday, but you'd be mistaken. The music may be out of fashion, but death and suffering have always served as a great excuse to write extremely affecting, deeply emotional music. No one today need apologize for buying tickets at any time of year to a performance of Requiems by Mozart, Verdi, Brahms, Fauré, Berlioz, or Britten, never mind Bach's Passions. Haydn's *The Seven Last Words of the Savior on the Cross*, in its comparatively colorless string quartet version, probably has more recordings to its credit than his true quartets. Misery, especially spiritual misery, sells, especially when joined to a message of ultimate salvation.

Bach's vocal works fall naturally into three basic categories: (1) songs, (2) sacred music for church performance, and (3) concert pieces both sacred and secular.

Songs

Bach composed songs throughout his life to both sacred and secular texts, more than 250 of them. He was on friendly terms with some of the major poets of his day, and was happy to collaborate in musical settings of their verses. Bach also took care to observe the musical culture and predilections of his audiences in Berlin and Hamburg. In the latter city, for example, in addition to running the major municipal musical organizations, he edited the periodical *Musikalisches Vielerley* (Musical Miscellany). This offered him a platform on which to publish individual songs and sonatas, as well as those by colleagues, with whom he maintained a mostly friendly competition. Bach's most important song collections contain settings of sacred poetry. Most of these are strophic: that is, there are several verses all sung to the same music.

Although technically intended for the amateur market, Bach was too much the musician not to include sometimes elaborate keyboard parts, with fully notated embellishments, and vocal lines more suited to singers possessed of at least some formal training. Several of the sacred songs were arranged as choruses with orchestra or inserted into Bach's liturgical works for performance in church. As such, they represent that practical flexibility that Bach and his contemporaries typically expected and exploited. In other words, this was music intended to be *used*, and Bach took its composition very seriously indeed.

Sacred Odes and Songs with Melodies, Wq 194 (Gellert Songs, 1758)
Twelve Sacred Odes and Songs with Melodies as an Appendix to Gellert's Sacred Odes and Songs with Melodies, Wq 195 (various authors, 1764)

It was only to be expected that Christian Fürchtgott Gellert (1715–69), a guy whose first name was "Christian" and whose middle name means "fear God," would publish a collection of sacred poetry. This he did in 1757, and Bach was so impressed with it that he set all fifty-four poems, apparently on his own initiative. The published composition, issued in 1758, turned out to be very popular, so much so that in later editions—five came out in his lifetime—he added an appendix of twelve new sacred songs by a miscellany of poets, some of whose names we do not know. Bach's preface reads, in part:

> In the preparation of the melodies I have, so far as possible, considered the entire Lied [song]. I say so far as possible because no one who understands music can be unaware that one must not require too much of a melody to which more than one strophe [verse] is sung, because the variety of the distinguishing marks, of the single- and multiple-syllable words, also often of the subject

> matter, etc. of the musical expression make a great difference. One will perceive from my work that I have sought in various ways to avoid many of these kinds of disparities.
>
> I have added to my melodies the necessary harmony and embellishments. Thus I did not leave them to the discretion of an inflexible figured-bass player, and, consequently one can use them as keyboard pieces. Since the voice part is always on top, untrained voices will thereby have a considerably easier experience.
>
> I deliver them in the order in which I wrote them. In a couple of Lieder I have, for variety, mixed in an expanded melodic idea. The words are thereby a bit more separated than usual; hopefully this circumstance will be as little of a stumbling block as in performed chorales where it is found even more often. The melodies before which one finds the words *lively*, *cheerful*, etc. require a moderate tempo—otherwise one can easily fall into a brash expression whereby he forgets that he has *spiritual* Lieder in front of him.[15]

As you can see Bach is hedging his bets a bit, because as always what counts, first and foremost, is the integrity of the musical experience. The idea of performing these songs as keyboard solos is very striking, as is the implication that for Bach *easy* means "doing what I say because I wrote it all down for you," and not "well suited to those with only meager talent." His concern to create variety, even in these restricted circumstances, is also telling and entirely characteristic. As for the songs themselves, it's useful to recall comedienne Anna Russell's description of the German Lied as "magnificent music set to rather soggy poetry." Here's a typical verse (with my own rough, unrhyming translation) out of a total of ten from the "Danklied" (Song of Thanks), No. 8 in the Gellert collection:

> Um Trost war meiner Seele so bang,
> denn Gott verbarg sein Angesicht,
> Ich rief zu ihm: Ach Herr, wie so lange?
> Und Gott verließ den Schwachen nicht.
> For comfort my fearful soul had need,
> Because God had hidden his face,
> I call to him, "O Lord, how much longer?"
> And God does not abandon the weak.

Cramer's Psalm Translations with Melodies, Wq 196 (1774)

Bach's next big collection of sacred songs consists of forty-two settings of Johann Andreas Cramer's (1723–88) free poetic German renderings of the biblical Psalms. Cramer actually translated all 150 Psalms, but as Bach explained in his preface,

> I have chosen only those Psalms that still suit our present time, and that serve for general devotion.
>
> In addition, I have had to leave out those that exhibit more than one meter, those that are too long to sing, those that are too variable in their content such that they would require a fuller treatment, and those with many alternating choruses, so that I could deliver to amateurs a not too large and expensive publication.[16]

Once again we see Bach's practicality combined with an emphasis on musical values, variety, and elements of his personal style (he goes on to note his preference for "adventurous modulations"). Of all the sacred song collections, these Psalm settings are probably the most viable today owing the universality of their texts. Indeed, they would make excellent additions to any sacred service in small congregations lacking substantial musical forces. All you need is a singer and a piano. Bach also reused some of these songs for the Psalm settings in some of his Passions.

Sturm's Sacred Songs with Melodies, Wq 197 and 198 (1780/81)

Christoph Christian Sturm (1740–86) was the pastor of St. Petri church in Hamburg, and a major force in the religious and intellectual life of the city. He was on friendly terms with Bach and the two collaborated in selecting the sixty poems, in groups of thirty, for the two volumes of songs that compose Wq 197 and 198. Sturm's poems cover a wide range of subjects, with an emphasis on the omnipresence of God the Creator in nature. There is a "four seasons" (well, three actually) of summer, autumn, and spring songs—and we can count the two Christmas songs for winter, if we like. Morning and evening get their due, and the second volume concludes with "The Sun." These pieces add variety to the expected songs of praise, of supplication, and reflection on the life, death, and resurrection of Jesus. Given the genre, then, these songs show an unusually wide range of subject matter, while frequent tempo designations, such as "Lebhaft" (swift, lively) and "Fröhlich" (joyful), point to their generally optimistic and contented character.

Odes with Melodies, Wq 199
New Song Melodies, Wq 200
Miscellaneous Collected Songs, Wq 201 and 202

All of Bach's remaining published songs are included in the above groups, and the only "leftovers" consist of a handful of pieces in manuscript, chorale tunes for congregational singing, and some alternate versions. The secular songs cover every genre: love songs, funeral songs, birthday songs, a couple of drinking songs, songs about nature, women, life, and art. There's even a fairly lengthy solo cantata, *Die Grazien* (The Graces), with recitatives, passages in aria style, and interludes for the keyboard. Taken together, these works made Bach not only one of the foremost songwriters of his day, they mark an important historical contribution to the development of the German Lied, a medium that came to full flowering in the work of Schubert some three decades after Bach's death. It's a repertoire that singers should consider exploring, and who knows? Maybe some of it will start to appear in recital programs once again now that the songs have been published in the Complete Works Edition.

Sacred Music for Church Performance

Let's put it this way: yes, it was great that all of those manuscripts from the Berlin Sing-Akademie were rediscovered and repatriated back to Germany, including Bach's twenty-plus Passion settings. On the other hand, we can't help but be just a tad disappointed that Bach's numerous Passions turned out to be mostly arrangements of earlier music, kind of an assortment of "Greatest Hits from Eighteenth-Century North German Passion Settings," if you can imagine such a thing. So the bad news is that there is very little original music there, but the good news is that we don't have to listen to twenty-plus Passion settings. I doubt even the most penitentially inclined concertgoers or record collectors could handle that. These works are mostly of interest only to Bach scholars and liturgical music specialists.

The decline of liturgical music generally in the second half of the eighteenth century has been attributed to many factors, among them changing patterns of musical patronage, the rise of the classical style based on the language of Italian comic opera, and the consequent de-emphasis on strict counterpoint and other hallmarks of the "serious" or "learned" type of music considered appropriate for worship. On the broader intellectual front, Bach himself witnessed at firsthand the Enlightenment disdain for organized religion: Frederick the Great was a poster child for the new thinking on this subject. Bach's Passion settings also pointed to another very relevant emergent pattern, namely the creation of a musical canon based on "classic" works of the past. With literally thousands of first-rate, liturgically uncontroversial church cantatas, Masses, and other pieces from which to choose, what was the point in writing new stuff, especially in a style increasingly seen as dated, for situations in which originality of content was the precise opposite of what was desired or appropriate?

Of course, Bach did write original sacred music. In 1749, as tradition has it, he composed the Magnificat, Wq 215, as an audition piece for his father's job in Leipzig. Failing to obtain the position, he revised the work around 1779, amplifying the scoring and replacing one of the movements. He had long since cannibalized the piece for use in his Passions and other church works, but in its final incarnation it became, like much of the rest of his sacred music, a concert piece as well as a liturgical one. The revised version was published in or about 1830 and it helped to keep his name alive throughout the nineteenth century. It is not only one of Bach's earliest surviving pieces of church music; it's the only one you really need to hear unless you're truly a hard-core collector.

As prayer settings go, the Magnificat offers more musical opportunities than most. Unlike the Mass, with its problematically doctrinaire central Credo and anticlimactic plea for peace at the end, the text is short, expressive, and it concludes with the convenient formula, "As it was in the beginning, so it is now and shall always be, forever and ever, Amen." This naturally suggests a recapitulation of the music from the opening, which is what J. S. Bach does. C. P. E. adopts a slightly different strategy. He brings back the initial music for the penultimate line, "Glory to the Father, the Son, and the Holy Spirit," and so the words of the concluding fugue ("As it was in the beginning," etc.) then explain why he did it—a very clever idea, you have to admit. The text itself represents Mary's celebratory prayer of thanks to God on learning that she will give birth to Jesus. It is, by turns, jubilant, humble, and reflective.

Bach's revised setting is scored for pairs of flutes, oboes, and horns, three trumpets, timpani, strings, continuo, four-part chorus, and the standard four vocal soloists (soprano, alto, tenor, bass). There are nine movements, lasting about forty minutes in total:

1. Magnificat anima mea (chorus)
2. Quia respexit humilitatem (soprano aria)
3. Quia fecit mihi magna (tenor aria)
4. Et misericordia eius (chorus)
5. Fecit potentiam (bass aria)
6. Deposuit potentes (alto and tenor duet)
7. Suscepit Israel (alto aria)
8. Gloria Patri (chorus, reprise of opening music)
9. Tutti: Sicut erat in principio (chorus)

In the later Hamburg version Bach wrote a new setting of the chorus "Et misericordia," possibly because he had reused the earlier one and when he revived the Magnificat for its later performances he didn't want to be heard repeating himself. Both are lovely, expressive pieces. The ritornellos that introduce the arias are classic C. P. E. Bach. That for "Fecit potentiam," especially, sounds like a major-key version of the opening of the Keyboard Concerto Wq 23. It features the same use of wide melodic intervals in leaping rhythms, the same alternation of loud and soft, and some very similar harmonic progressions. If indeed the work was designed to show off what Bach could do as a composer of church music, it definitely delivers the goods, but it also makes an ideal concert work both in terms of length and variety of expressive content.

There are numerous other works that Bach composed for liturgical purposes: cantatas, the two Litanies, Wq 204, motets for choir, Psalm settings, and the like. Many of them have been recorded and can be sampled at leisure. As I mentioned previously, we are still in the early days of sifting through so much of Bach's output, the vocal works especially, and only time will tell which pieces continue to speak to us in a meaningful way. Merely by listening you become an active participant in this grand, evolving historical process.

Sacred and Secular Concert Pieces

As the history of the Magnificat shows, the boundaries between the sacred and the secular in the eighteenth century could be quite fuzzy. At least two of Bach's three oratorios began life as liturgical pieces, but wound up as concert works. The performance of music on sacred subjects outside of churches can be said to have marked the beginning of the view of concert halls as "temples of art" dedicated to what ultimately became the secular religion of music. This perspective grew increasingly powerful throughout the nineteenth century, and it greatly helped in removing a certain suspicion—particularly among the middle class—that always attached to music on account of its more sensuous qualities, never mind the dubious profession of musician in the first place. The use of music as an active source of moral improvement, harnessing and directing the passions in contemplation of the basic tenets of the Christian faith, underlies most of Bach's vocal output, and perhaps "rubbed off" on his instrumental music as well.

The famous benefit concert that Bach gave in Hamburg in 1786 offers a case in point. On the first half he presented the Credo from his father's B-Minor Mass alongside two movements from Handel's *Messiah*: the aria "I know that my redeemer liveth," and the Hallelujah Chorus. The second half featured his own music: a symphony, the Magnificat, and the glorious *Heilig*, Wq 217, for two choirs and two orchestras. At this concert Bach revealed the continuity of purpose found in his own works, both sacred and secular, as the logical successors to iconic musical exemplars of faith and spirituality.

Lasting only about five or six minutes, the *Heilig* also began life as a church piece. In preparing the work for publication in 1778, Bach wrote to his publisher, "this *Heilig* is an attempt to inspire far greater attention and sentiment through entirely natural and ordinary harmonic progressions than one can attain with any amount of nervous chromaticism. It is to be my swan song of this type, and thereby serve the purpose that I may not be forgotten too soon after my death."[17] The piece consists of a brief Ariette for alto soloist to set the scene, followed by the same words (in German) that form the Sanctus section of the Latin Mass: "Holy, Holy, Holy, Lord God of hosts. Heaven and earth are full of Thy glory!" The text comes from Isaiah 6:3, and the two choirs represent angels and "the people." Bach was pretty obviously inspired by Handel's Hallelujah Chorus, or perhaps "Zadok the Priest" from the Coronation Anthems, and for a short work the one packs a big punch.

His most important vocal compositions, however, are the three oratorios. Bach was tremendously proud of them. There is no stronger evidence of this than the fact that Bach arranged to have *Die Israeliten in der Wüste* and *Die Auferstehung und Himmelfahrt Jesu* published in full score, at considerable financial risk. Regarding the latter, Bach stated, "I can nevertheless claim, without ridiculous egotism, that it will wear well for many years, because it is among my masterpieces an important one, from which young composers can learn something."[18] The earliest of the three, however, is the Passion Cantata, also variously known as *Die letzten Leiden des Erlösers* (The Last Sorrows of the Savior) or *Du Göttlicher* (Ye Godly), which began life as one of Bach's Passion settings—so you probably know the story already.

Like most of Bach's works, especially that ones that he published, the oratorios were revised over the years and all of the borrowings, whether from himself or anyone else, were eliminated until only original material remains. This, of course, made good marketing sense; no purchaser wanted to spend good money on used music dressed up with different words. More significantly, however, is Bach's repeated claim that he wished to secure his name for posterity; and so as for most composers of his day (Haydn included), his surest bet was by writing popular vocal music. Indeed, his oratorios did extremely well. *Die Auferstehung*, notably, made a big splash in Vienna, courtesy of Baron van Swieten, in performance versions arranged by Mozart, no less, while the Passion Cantata received annual performances in Hamburg for many years.

Aside from Graun's *Der Tod Jesu*, the proximate model for Bach's oratorios was Handel's *Messiah*. They are not dramatic works, effectively operas for the concert platform, nor are they terribly lengthy—no longer than your average Mahler symphony, say, seventy-five to ninety minutes apiece. Instead, they present a series of biblical scenes on which the soloists and chorus comment with music emotionally expressive of the events being described. For example, in the first part of *Die Israeliten*, the chorus laments its seemingly endless wanderings and fears that God has turned away from His chosen people. They reproach Moses for their misfortune. Moses prays to God for relief, water flows from the rocks, and the people rejoice accordingly. The second part is mostly a joyful series of numbers in praise of God and the promise of future redemption.

Bach was not fond of musical illustration, if by that we mean "imitation of some nonmusical sound," but he was extremely sensitive to the meaning of his texts, both emotionally and pictorially. When the water flows, so do the notes in the violins. His orchestration, for the same basic forces we find in the revised Magnificat, is consistently colorful and appropriate to the context. While drama in the sense of "action" is lacking in these works, as it is Handel's *Messiah*, the arias are typically affecting, and some of the choruses are thrilling. The concluding number of *Die Auferstehung* is a choral extravaganza nearly ten minutes long with multiple tempos, meters, textures and tonalities, and some rather amazing (for the period) solo trumpet writing. It's a real pity that it's not better known, and a pity too that space forbids discussing these pieces in greater detail. Fortunately, all of them have been recorded—very well, too—and while you may not need all three, you may want to sample at least the two that Bach himself took the time and trouble to publish. He knew their value, and was a good judge of his own work.

This "vocal interlude" concludes with one of Bach's last and most delightful short vocal pieces, his 1783 setting of Friedrich Klopstock's catchily titled *Morgengesang am Schöpfungsfeste*, Wq 239 (Morning Song at the Festival of the Creation). Klopstock (1724–1803) was one of the major German poets of his day, and a friend of Bach's. He is best known today in musical circles as the author of the "Resurrection Ode" set to music by Mahler as the finale of his eponymous Second Symphony. The text that Bach selected treats the rising of the sun on the first day of the newly created Earth as a metaphor for the immortality of the soul and the promise of resurrection. Both mankind and the sun are equally children of God. Klopstock's vision of God manifest in nature is classic Enlightenment philosophy, and it offered Bach the opportunity to write music that's consistently interesting and affecting even though it never turns dark or tragic.

Bach's setting requires a chamber ensemble of two flutes and strings, plus continuo. The text is divided up between two sopranos and the chorus. There are nine numbers that play continuously, accelerating in tempo and liveliness until the final sunrise. The entire piece lasts only ten to twelve minutes, and it's quite astonishing how much variety C. P. E. packs into the music. He begins with an accompanied recitative, followed by an arioso, an aria, a duet, a chorus, another duet, another accompanied recitative, and a final chorus with soloists. The longest number is the first, a bit more than two minutes, while the compactness of the rest makes the steady increase in energy evocative of daybreak without ever becoming overly literal. This is Bach, or at least one side of his personality, in a nutshell. The piece has been recorded a few times, and can be found on discs devoted to his vocal works more generally.

I hope that this brief survey provides a taste of Bach's vocal output that will serve as a useful guide for future listening. It only remains for the musicologists, concert organizations, and record labels to do their part.

Part 3

Solo Instrumental and Chamber Music

7 Keyboard Music

General Introduction

> *Especially in the last few years, I have been turning my attention to playing the clavier, and composing for it, as lyrically as possible, despite the impossibility of sustaining notes. This matter is not at all easy if one does not want to leave the ear empty or spoil the noble simplicity of song by too much noise.*
>
> *It seems to me that music must first and foremost stir the heart, and a clavier player can never achieve this by mere pounding, drumming, and arpeggiating—at least not for me.*
>
> —C. P. E. Bach, *Autobiography* [19]

In considering C. P. E. Bach's production for keyboard instruments we come to the core of his output—the field in which he specialized and really had no peer during his lifetime. He wrote around three hundred pieces for this medium, many of which were published, and many of which were not. About half fall into the category of "sonata." Bach saw approximately a hundred of those published in his lifetime. The rest consist of rondos, fantasies, variations, dances, character pieces, and miscellaneous short works for teaching and practice. It is, by any standard, an extremely impressive body of work, equaled perhaps only by the 555 keyboard sonatas of Domenico Scarlatti. However, as we shall see, a sonata for Scarlatti and a sonata for Bach were very different things.

Table 3: Keyboard Works

Wq or H #	Title (# of pieces in collection)	Translations/Notes
Wq 42	Keyboard Concerto in F Major	Version for keyboard solo
Wq 43	Six Keyboard Concertos	Versions for keyboard solo
Wq 48	Prussian Sonatas (6)	
Wq 49	Württemberg Sonatas (6)	
Wq 50	Sechs Sonaten für Clavier mit veränderten Reprisen	Six Keyboard Sonatas with Varied Reprises
Wq 51	Fortsetzung von sechs Sonaten fürs Clavier	Sequel of Six Keyboard Sonatas
Wq 52	Zweyte Fortsetzung von sechs Sonaten fürs Clavier	Second Sequel of Six Keyboard Sonatas
Wq 53	Sechs leichte Clavier-Sonaten	Six Easy Keyboard Sonatas
Wq 54	Six Sonates pour le Clavecin, à l'usage des Dames	Six Keyboard Sonatas for Ladies
Wq 55	Sechs Clavier-Sonaten für Kenner und Liebhaber; Erste Sammlung	Six Keyboard Sonatas for Connoisseurs and Amateurs; First Volume
Wq 56	Clavier-Sonaten nebst einigen Rondos fürs Fortepiano für Kenner und Liebhaber; Zweyte Sammlung (6)	Sonatas and Rondos for Fortepiano for Connoisseurs and Amateurs; Second Volume
Wq 57	Clavier-Sonaten nebst einigen Rondos fürs Fortepiano für Kenner und Liebhaber; Dritte Sammlung (6)	Sonatas and Rondos for Fortepiano for Connoisseurs and Amateurs; Third Volume
Wq 58	Clavier-Sonaten und freye Fantasien, nebst einigen Rondos fürs Fortepiano, für Kenner und Liebhaber; Vierte Sammlung (7)	Sonatas, Free Fantasias, and Rondos for Connoisseurs and Amateurs; Fourth Volume
Wq 59	Clavier-Sonaten und freye Fantasien nebst einigen Rondos fürs Fortepiano, für Kenner und Liebhaber; Fünfte Sammlung (6)	Sonatas, Free Fantasias, and Rondos for Connoisseurs and Amateurs; Fifth Volume

continued

Wq or H #	Title (# of pieces in collection)	Translations/Notes
Wq 60	Sonata in C Minor	
Wq 61	Clavier-Sonaten und freye Fantasien nebst einigen Rondos fürs Fortepiano für Kenner und Liebhaber; Sechste Sammlung (6)	Sonatas, Free Fantasias, and Rondos for Connoisseurs and Amateurs; Sixth Volume
Wq 62	Clavier-Sonaten die in verschiedenen Sammlungen einzeln gedruckt stehen (24)	Keyboard Sonatas Published Individually in Various Volumes
Wq 63	Sechs Sonaten zu Versuche über die wahre Art das Clavier zu spielen; nebst sechs neue Sonatinen (Probestücke)	Six Sonatas for the Essay on the True Method of Keyboard Playing; with Six New Sonatinas (Practice-pieces)
Wq 64	Sechs Sonatinen für das Clavier	Six Keyboard Sonatinas
Wq 65	Vollständige Sammlung aller ungedruckte Clavier-Sonaten (50)	Complete Volume of All Unpublished Keyboard Sonatas (incl. Suite in E Minor, Wq 65/4)
Wq 66	Abschied von meinem Silbermannischen Claviere, in einem Rondo	Farewell to My Silbermann Clavichord, in a Rondo (Rondo in E Minor)
Wq 67	Freie Fantasie fürs Clavier "Carl Philipp Emanuel Bachs Empfindungen"	Free Fantasia for Keyboard in F-sharp Minor "Carl Philipp Emanuel Bach's Emotions" (also arr. for violin and keyboard, Wq 80)
Wq 68	Varied and embellished versions of selected sonatas	
Wq 69	Sonata in D Minor	For harpsichord with two manuals (keyboards)
Wq 70	Six Sonatas and One Prelude for Organ	
Wq 79	Arioso with 5 Variations in A Major	Version for solo keyboard of Trio in A Major

continued

Wq or H #	Title (# of pieces in collection)	Translations/Notes
Wq 111	Menuet pour le Clavessin	Minuet for Harpsichord (1731) [1st Printed Work]
Wq 112	Clavierstücke verschiedener Art (19)	Keyboard Pieces of Various Types
Wq 113	Kurze und leichte Clavierstücke mit veränderten Reprisen, Erste Sammlung (11)	Short and Easy Keyboard Pieces with Varied Reprises, First Volume
Wq 114	Kurze und leichte Clavierstücke mit veränderten Reprisen, Zweyte Sammlung (11)	Short and Easy Keyboard Pieces with Varied Reprises, Second Volume
Wq 115	Vier kleine Duetten für zwei Claviere	Four Little Duets for Two Keyboards
Wq 116	Sammlung von Menuetten, Polonaisen und andern Handstücken fürs Clavier (28)	Volume of Minuets, Polonaises, and Different Pieces for Keyboard
Wq 117	Sammlung von Solfeggios, Fantasien und charakteristische Stücke fürs Clavier (40)	Volume of Solfeggios, Fantasias and Character Pieces for Keyboard
Wq 118	Sammlung verschiedener Clavierstücke mit Variationen (10)	Volume of Various Keyboard Pieces with Variations
Wq 119/2-7	Six Fugues for Organ	
Wq 120	Cadenzas for concertos and sonatas	
Wq 122/1-3	Symphonies in G Major, F Major, E Minor	Versions for solo keyboard
Wq 122/5	Symphony in F Major	Version for solo keyboard
Wq 199/16	"L'Ernestine"	
H 1/1-4	Four Pieces for Anna Magdalena Bach (1730)	2 marches and 2 polonaises
H 255	Allegro in D Major	
H 256	Allegro in F Major	

continued

Wq or H #	Title (# of pieces in collection)	Translations/Notes
H 257	Allegretto in D Major	
H 258	Menuett in F Major	
H 336	Five Organ Chorales	
H 340	Polonaise in G Major	
H 348	Fantasia in E-flat Major	

In assembling his catalog, Wotquenne generally respected the integrity of the editions that Bach published himself, and then agglomerated everything else into groups consisting, for example, of all of the unpublished sonatas, Wq 65, or the volumes of miscellaneous pieces, Wq 116 and 117. These three collections alone contain over a hundred individual works. Given this abundance of riches, there is no way to give a detailed description of everything, but we will survey some highlights from all of the major sets, in order by Wotquenne number, so that you can plan your own listening and get a good sense of what to expect. We also will spend some time describing the works for solo keyboard whose recordings come with this book. First, however, a bit of history will put things in context.

Bach lived at a time of remarkable evolution in the history of keyboard instruments. The piano was slowly replacing the harpsichord as the king of this particular family. The clavichord was enjoying a spurt of popularity, and a whole host of new and peculiar musical gadgets appeared and vanished over the course of the eighteenth century. Indeed, Bach composed the Sonata in G Major, Wq 65/48, for a *Bogen-Clavier* (bowed harpsichord), a contraption whole principal claim to fame was that it could sustain tones like a string instrument and produce some semblance of a vocal vibrato, like a violin or clavichord.

Why was this so important? Bach's own comments at the head of this chapter suggest the reason. The ability to imitate the human voice remained the acme of instrumental achievement for him as for all of his contemporaries. Keyboard instruments had only recently achieved solo status, and musicians as well as builders were anxious to try anything that would improve their rather dubious qualifications as vocally expressive devices. The ability to sustain a sound was one of these, and to sustain that sound with vibrato—that natural, slight wavering of pitch that gives the voice its expressive warmth and varies accordingly to intensity—was very much a sort of musical Holy Grail. The clavichord, a small instrument that featured metal tangents striking the strings, could do it if the player wiggled the key gently after pressing it down. The harpsichord, and later the piano, could not.

Germans called this effect *Bebung* (trembling) when used on individual long notes, and *Tragen der Töne* (carrying the tone, or *portato* in Italian) for repeated notes and scales, but the clavichord was severely restricted in volume and thus limited to private performances in small rooms. Nevertheless, C. P. E. Bach loved the instrument for its enhanced expressive potential, so much so that he composed Wq 66, "Farewell to My Silberman Clavichord, in a Rondo" when he sold off his favorite model. This is one of the very few pieces that we know for sure was composed for the clavichord because it contains specific notation asking for vibrato. Eventually, the piano became Bach's instrument of choice for less intimate pieces on account of its expanded dynamic range and sustaining power, but the exemplars available to Bach at the end of his life in the 1780s had nothing like the sound of the models available today.

Composers in Bach's time, both for practical and commercial reasons, had to hedge their bets and write music that was playable on whatever happened to be available. Even the German word *Clavier* simply meant any kind of keyboard instrument, although it could also refer specifically to the clavichord (as is likely in Bach's comment at the head of this chapter). We do know that Bach's early preferred medium was the harpsichord, for his published works at least, and for his concertos. There is a certain myth that harpsichords have a severely limited dynamic range, and many of them do, but the larger models with double keyboards and "special effects," such a lute stops and the like, can produce a wide and interesting spectrum of tone colors and volume levels. Bach always tended to indicate precisely a full range of dynamics in his scores, even for those works clearly intended to be played on the harpsichord, and in his earliest collections—the "Prussian" and

"Württemberg" sonatas—his indications range from *pianissimo* (*pp*) to *forte* (*f*).

So, the bottom line is this: Bach's keyboard music can be played, and made to sound well, on just about anything that sounds well itself. Nevertheless, those listeners used to the sonority of a modern grand piano, with its big, fat, thrilling chords, may be disappointed. Nineteenth-century listeners found the piano writing of Bach (and Mozart, and Haydn) unacceptably thin. Much of Bach's keyboard writing involves just two parts. This stems partially from the often contrapuntal nature of the textures, but also from the fact that big, fat, thrilling chords on the harpsichord can sound more like a car with severe engine knock than they do music. Harpsichords are notoriously noisy instruments mechanically, so composers tended to compensate for the difficulty of writing thick textures by writing in a more linear fashion. The harpsichord also had no peer in Bach's day (or ours, for that matter) when it came to playing brilliant runs in quick tempos, or splashy figurations with lots of notes.

As you explore Bach's keyboard music, you may well encounter much discussion in booklet notes, online forums, and other places about which instrument he may have intended at different times in his career, or which best suits the work in question. "Historically informed" players often insist on their choice being "right," while scholars agonize over the relative merits of harpsichords, clavichords, fortepianos, tangent pianos (sort of a cross between a harpsichord and a piano), organs, and the numerous other options available at the time. Here's the truth: it usually doesn't matter. A great performance speaks for itself.

One of the more remarkable things about Bach's music is just how modern it sounds when played on modern instruments, whereas on early instruments it often sounds, well, like modern music being played on early instruments. His harmonic freedom has a lot to do with it, but the fact is that a lot of his writing just strikes the listener as timeless. It hasn't dated at all. This is very different from the impression produced by, say, his father's keyboard pieces, which have become iconic exemplars of baroque style, just as Mozart's embody the classical aesthetic. C. P. E.'s keyboard pieces sound like C. P. E., and that's about it. Sometimes, it seems, if your voice truly is original, it's a good thing to fall between periods, belonging completely to neither.

The music that accompanies this book contains examples of the three major forms that occupied Bach throughout his career, and feature most prominently in his keyboard works: sonata, rondo, and fantasia (or fantasy). We will discuss them now, in order of increasing complexity.

Rondo in B-flat Major, Wq 58 No. 5 (1779)

Allegro

We already have some experience with rondo form, since it features in both the Solfeggio and "L'Aly Rupalich," both previously discussed. At its simplest, the rondo has a basic ABACA shape, but it can have any number of episodes between returns of the rondo theme and thus the pattern can be indefinitely extended. Typically rondos occur as movements in larger works, including sonatas and concertos, but the freestanding rondo was very popular in Bach's day, and so he decided to add several to his final published collections in the *Kenner und Liebhaber* (Connoisseurs and Amateurs) series, as well as writing such works as the "Farewell" Rondo, Wq 66, mentioned earlier.

In the Viennese classics, rondos usually appear as quick finales, but C. P. E.'s can be slow or fast, happy or quite sad. Bach being Bach, he wasn't about to take on the challenge until he figured out how to "Bach-isize" the form, and so his rondos add a few twists to the basic idea. Given his love of contrast and variation, Bach seldom repeats the main theme, or ritornello, literally, but varies it whenever it returns, sometimes considerably. He also likes to write lots of short little episodes, in a wide variety of keys, tempos, and moods. The Rondo in B-flat Major, Wq 58/5, is a typical example of a quick piece in which all of these strategies come into play. It has the following shape:

- A (actually a miniature aba form, so you get to hear the main theme unvaried twice)
- B
- A (in a lower position)
- C

- A
- D (in a minor key, first slow then quick and virtuosic)
- A (still in the minor)
- E (transition back to the major)
- A
- F (back to the minor)
- A (minor)
- G (transition back to the major with reference to the fast music of D)
- A
- H (slow episode)
- A (in same slow tempo, mostly)
- D (recapitulation and extended variation of the earlier episode)
- A (varied and expanded into a dreamy and poetic cadenza/coda)

As you can see, there's a lot going on here, especially for a piece that lasts less than six minutes, but the form itself is very straightforward. The rondo theme (or ritornello) is quite short—only about nine seconds—and extremely catchy. It also comes to a full stop on an emphatic descending scale before continuing, something that you can't count on as a rule in other rondos, but which makes it even easier to get into your head in this particular case. Although the basic key of the piece is a cheerful B-flat major, Bach introduces sadder and more reflective emotions by spending a lot of time in minor keys, and also by reducing the tempo from fast to slow. The actual ending, in which the music floats away romantically in tranquil, rhythmically free keyboard figurations, comes as quite a surprise after everything that has occurred.

Another important feature is the importance of the D episode. A tiny recollection of D appears as part of episode G, and Bach recapitulates the entire section more fully toward the end. He clearly felt the need to firm up the structure given the music's expressive variety, and a bit of additional repetition, even though modified and developed further, provides an enhanced level of logical continuity. You may also note that bits of the ritornello, especially the rhythm of its first three notes and the melodic turn at the end of its first phrase, come and go within the individual episodes. In these ways a piece that risks sounding highly sectionalized achieves a striking level of musical unity despite its diversity of affect. As always with Bach, brevity never means a lack of depth or lower standards of craftsmanship.

Fantasia in F-sharp Minor, Wq 67 "C. P. E. Bach's Feelings" (1787)

Adagio

Composed in the year before his death, Bach's Fantasia in F-sharp Minor is one of his darkest works. Since the entire point of writing a fantasia in the first place is to capture the free form of an improvisation, I am not going to outline the shape of the piece other than to say that it consists of three distinct kinds of music:

1. A funeral march in strict time, a rhythm and series of harmonies without real melody, which makes it sound even starker and more forbidding then it otherwise would. Chopin's famous funeral march from his Second Sonata isn't far away in mood.
2. Melodic figuration that's very sad, and very speechlike and free, almost in recitative style. At times the feeling of words being spoken dissolves into more songlike passages. If the funeral march consists of rhythm without melody, then here we have its antithesis: melody without—or in any event with less—rhythm.
3. Fast and virtuosic outbursts featuring runs and scales up and down the keyboard.

These three kinds of music alternate and intermingle as the work proceeds, so there is plenty of recapitulation, always varied, over the twelve minutes or so that Bach requires. The precise details of this haunting, very beautiful, and very sad piece I leave to you to discover. Given the personal significance that the music must have had for him, it might not surprise you to learn that he also arranged it for violin and keyboard (as Wq 80), and comparison between the two versions is quite interesting since the gain in expressiveness through use of the violin has to be offset by the more rigid rhythmic framework that the duet format requires. I discuss this version, which contains one other very surprising difference, in the next chapter.

Sonata in F Minor, Wq 57 No. 6 (1763)

1. Allegro assai
2. Andante
3. Andantino grazioso

If Haydn became known as "the father of the symphony and string quartet," then by rights Bach should get credit as "the father of the sonata," for his series of keyboard sonatas represent the first modern works in the form that we would recognize as such. Scarlatti's sonatas, for example, are all almost all single-movement pieces falling neatly into two halves, both repeated. With Bach, we get the new model: multi-movement pieces usually lasting from eight to twelve minutes, at least one part of which adopts what later came to be called "sonata form." This means a binary (two-part) movement in which the first half contains an exposition of thematic material, moving away from the home key of the opening. The second half then develops that material through a process of variation and transformation, arriving at a recapitulation of the original ideas, now recast as necessary to remain in the initial key. This, at least, is the usual textbook view. The reality, as always in music, is a bit messier, but the general concept is valid enough.

What, then, does Bach's version of sonata form look like? Actually, it's quite simple. The above textbook view states that the "exposition" usually contains two clearly defined subjects, one in each of two major key areas, or tonalities. Bach's music is often so harmonically free, and his expositions so short and packed with distinctive motives of all different shapes and sizes, that it's easier not worry about which bit belongs to which "subject." Just think of the first half as a whole and leave it at that. Also, given his dislike of literal repetition, the process of "development" often starts right away, at least to the extent that this involves variations of the initial ideas. We saw this in the Sonata in C Minor discussed in the chapter "Listening to C. P. E.," although that work, formally, is actually a set of variations.

The result of these personal characteristics is that a typical movement in sonata form, for Bach, generally contains three more or less full statements of the exposition. The first, often repeated and itself varied, presents the initial themes and motives and gradually leaves the home key (or tonic); the second develops these ideas—usually with Bach in the same order—and works its way back to the tonic, while the third reprises the opening, but in such a way that the tonic gets reinforced to form a satisfying close. This will be the case where Bach's intention is to arrive at the end, but as we have seen in connection with the symphonies, there are many times when he does not want to stop. Rather, if there are additional movements to come, he may jump suddenly to the next movement without warning, or gradually effect a transition. These situations add spice and variety, but they don't really change the basic principle.

This is just one kind of sonata form, and as you can see it's pretty straightforward, and even easier to hear than it is to describe. There are a couple of other versions, and happily the Sonata in F Minor, Wq 57/6, offers an example of each.

This work, which Bach published in the third volume of his *Kenner und Liebhaber* series, was very highly regarded during his lifetime, and it even became one of the very few pieces to enjoy a publication and revival during the nineteenth century. We will discuss matters of shape and structure in some detail because these questions are always important in considering music in larger forms such as this sonata, but then I am going to ask you to forget all about them because, ultimately, formal consideration offers little more than scaffolding supporting what really matters for Bach: the immediacy of emotional expression.

First Movement: Allegro assai

The driving opening theme of this splendid movement features a leaping figure in dotted rhythm, and has a distinctive ABA shape to it. Remember those dotted rhythms and the general shape of the tune, because every movement begins in a similar way, even though the principal melody in each will turn out to be distinctive. Indeed, you can make a good case that all of the movements start with a variation of the first, and whether you recognize the fact consciously or not the result is a strong feeling of unity that joins the three movements into a coherent whole. Subtle binding elements such as these give Bach's music much of its life and depth, and they became a very important aspect of the Viennese classical style.

It just so happens that this movement represents an absolutely perfect example of Bach's personal use of sonata form. The exposition contains three ideas: that initial theme just mentioned, a rapid passage featuring even quarter notes over a steady triplet rhythm (a triplet is three notes squeezed into the space of two), and a loud, strange, syncopated sequence of chords that starts with a bang. The exposition ends with an abbreviated review of all three of these ideas in rapid succession. It plays for about fifty seconds. The whole passage is then repeated from the beginning with whatever modifications and ornaments the player cares to add, if any.

Most of Bach's development sections start with his opening theme, and this one is no exception, only now the tune appears in a jaunty major key. The music follows the course of the exposition, moving on to those flowing triplets, which surprisingly keep right on flowing. The loud, syncopated motive plays no part here. Instead, Bach turns on a geyser that gushes up from the depths of the keyboard, and in a series of amazingly gorgeous modulations more typical of Debussy than of anything obviously eighteenth century, those persistent triplets lead us in a flash back to F minor and the start of the recapitulation.

It's important to understand what just happened here. The moment that leads back to the tonic key offers a creative opportunity. Bach can stick close to the order of events in the exposition, which he sometimes does, or he can compose a sort of bridge or transition either based on new material or on some transformation of an idea from the exposition. In this case, the constant feature is the flowing triplet rhythm, but the harmonic scheme is entirely daring and new, and because of that the return of the opening theme has a very gratifying feeling of "arrival" from a point far away. When listening to a Bach sonata, try to pay particular attention to moments such as these. They offer endless opportunities to hear with what inexhaustible imagination Bach invests his approach to this basic formal procedure.

The recapitulation follows the entire exposition in its original order, except for the fact that now the music remains in its home key of F minor, and one other interesting point. You will recall that the opening theme originally had an ABA shape, and if you were listening carefully you might have noticed that the second "A" was lightly varied—just a few little ornaments for variety's sake. Now, it just so happens that "A" consists of two identical phrases. This means that for the recapitulation Bach can *combine* both ways of playing them, first the original, then the variation for the second phrase. It's a subtle but highly characteristic little touch, and I have always thought that when a composer who operates at this level of detail tells the performer, "Sure, go ahead and ornament if you like," then the player had better think twice before taking up the invitation.

More significantly, Bach will do exactly the same thing—that is, play the "A" bit of the initial theme only once at the recapitulation—in the next two movements. He can do this because, as I mentioned, the remaining principal themes have the same basic shape. Once again we have evidence of a deeper level of unity at work. The reason I am stressing this point will become evident shortly.

Finally, we leave the first movement after considering the sometimes-vexatious question of repeats. Until Haydn's late symphonies, most sonata form movements in the eighteenth century remained faithful to their binary routes and indicated that both halves (that is, exposition and development/recapitulation) should be repeated. There were exceptions, notably in concertos because of the presence of the soloist, but in symphonies and other instrumental works two halves, both repeated, was the standard. Performers always have the option to obey or ignore this directive, and it really depends on the work. Often the player will observe the exposition repeat and ignore that for the second half for the simple reason that it sounds lame to modern ears to hear a piece end, and then start up again from the middle.

This became a real problem in Viennese classical music because of the strongly dramatic tonal tensions that get resolved with such impressive finality at the very end. Very few composers, Haydn aside, wrote pieces that make something convincing of second-half repeats, and even he finally abandoned them. As I observed in discussing the concertos, the "grand finale" is less of an issue for Bach because his style does not rely on the idea of climactic final bars as the ultimate goal to which the music has been heading, and so his endings are often pointedly abrupt. In this particular sonata, observing all the repeats results in a perfectly balanced work in which each movement is almost exactly the same length: between four and five minutes. Given the relationship between the movements on other levels, we can only believe that fidelity to Bach's requests to take a repeat is highly desirable.

Second Movement: Andante

There are no big sectional repeats in this movement, and when the usual tripartite sonata form lacks them and the development section, as here, contains a lot of new-sounding material, then the form often comes across as a big ABA. If you listen to the opening gesture you will recognize the same leaping figures in dotted rhythm from the beginning of the first movement; and as already mentioned, the overall shape of theme is similar. The emotional ambiance, however, couldn't be more different. If the first movement was stern, athletic and bold, this tune is jovial and perhaps a touch pompous. However, it doesn't remain that way.

In music, slow often means big, and much of this movement consists of development. The section begins, as in the first movement, with the opening theme, but the mood swiftly darkens as the music turns toward gloomy, minor keys and to melodic material seemingly unrelated to the principal themes. The bridge passage contains the darkest music yet, but the dotted-note gesture in the left hand hints at where the music is headed. Unlike previously, however, where we arrived back in the tonic with great energy and logic, here the melody simply fades out and stops, seemingly in the middle of nowhere. Then Bach begins the recapitulation in the home key as if nothing had happened.

Of course, something *has* happened, something unresolved. You can hear Bach transpose the music of the exposition and beginning of the development into the original major key, and it seems as though the music will close tranquilly after all. Suddenly the harmony darkens once again, turning resolutely to the minor, and gradually comes to a halt, but not to a conclusion. Instead, after an unresolved chord, Bach continues straight on to the finale, confirming not the major key of this Andante but rather the original home key of F minor.

Third Movement: Andantino grazioso

The tempo of this movement, a "gracious little andante," is slow to moderate, but flowing. You might think that two movements similar in speed would lead to monotony, but their characters are very different. The Andante just heard is full of loud, jerky rhythms and short motives. This finale, despite the unifying dotted rhythms evident in the opening bars, displays a smoothly singing lyricism quite different from anything heard thus far. Although not without occasional outbursts, the dynamic level remains subdued, the mood sad but not tragic or hysterical—perhaps regretful and nostalgic.

During this period, slow finales were virtually unheard of, slow finales ending in minor keys even more so. The point, however, is not that the music is slow, but rather that it feels emotionally *right*. This is why I emphasized earlier the formal connections between the various movements. It is true that Bach's music shows a great variety of affect, but we always need to keep in mind Bach's overriding purpose, which is to display these feelings truthfully, naturally and convincingly. In a large movement or multi-sectional work, it isn't just the moment-to-moment emotions that need to convince, but also the *sequence* in which they appear. Bach attends to both of these necessities. There is an overarching story here: the evolution of a human personality, from gruffness and striving, through a certain false bravado pierced by moments of insecurity, to a sense of resigned sadness fortified by moments of consolation. This goes way beyond the usual "major = happy, minor = sad" construct, taking the music to a higher and more complex level of emotional sophistication.

The form of this very beautiful finale supports the above interpretation. It has two halves, both repeated, and can best be described as "sonata without development." The two halves are, in fact, mirror images of each other. The first half moves from a pathetic minor to a more hopeful major, and the second half reverses the process. This means that the recapitulation begins in the major, and the second half repeat, which reaffirms the music's path from light to darkness, only deepens the pathos of the final bars. The music has that timeless quality that we find so often in Bach's work, and which arises from his handling large-scale form in a way that conveys an expressive message words can't adequately describe—but that we feel instinctively to be true.

Before moving on to consideration of the individual keyboard music collections in the next chapter, I should mention one more significant point applicable to Bach's music in general, and to his keyboard works in particular. This concerns their often-remarked unpredictability and variety, and their relation to the ideal of vocal music. In 1783, Bach's friend and colleague Carl Friedrich Cramer, editor of the *Magazin der Musik,* published in article in which he discusses the use of vibrato in instrumental music, noting, "If vocal performance and the expression of passionate emotion are the models and ideal for the instrument (to the extent that the indefinite wordless tone permits), then it goes without saying that the instrumentalist, in places where the voice would use vibrato, not only may use it, but must."

All other issues of personal style aside, if we generalize from Cramer's specific case in point, he offers the justification for the extremes of intensity and unpredictability to which Bach's music aspires, and which continue to fascinate us today. The bottom line is this: music without words has to exaggerate its expressive characteristics in order to achieve the same level of communicative clarity that texted music enjoys relatively effortlessly—at least, that was the rationale in the composer's time. The reason it's important to understand this is because the best way to listen and appreciate these pieces is not to regard Bach as an outrageous or revolutionary anarchist flouting musical convention and "the rules" gratuitously, but rather as a virtuoso composer whose flamboyant technique employs certain effects deliberately in order to underline the music's expressive meaning.

Think of the dialogue in a play: it can run fast or slow, loud or soft, be punctuated by dramatic accents, shouts, whispers, ironic asides, and sudden changes of subject or digressions. All of these have their equivalents in Bach's music. This can be easier to hear in the concertos and symphonies because their larger resources, and especially the opposition between solo and ensemble, make it easier to achieve broad contrasts. But the laboratory in which Bach put his aesthetic to most intensive use is that of his output for solo keyboard. Other composers, notably his father, had shown that instrumental music could be as richly fulfilling as writing for voices, but it was C. P. E. who made the best case for regarding music without words as equally meaningful, because in his hands its range of expression and variety of affect became as diverse as music with a text.

Guide to the Collections of Pieces

"Prussian" Sonatas, Wq 48 (1742)

No. 1 in F Major
No. 2 in B-flat Major
No. 3 in E Major
No. 4 in C Minor
No. 5 in C Major
No. 6 in A Major

Bach did not always write new works specifically for publication. Often he would draw on his stock of preexisting music and "polish it up" as necessary, and he composed at least fifteen sonatas (and the six sonatinas Wq 64) before writing these pieces in 1740 and 1741. However, this collection really was conceived as a cohesive set, which makes sense when you consider, first, that Frederick the Great was the dedicatee, and second, Bach clearly wanted to offer evidence of what he could do with the form in this, his first major opus offered to the public. We have no idea, actually, what Frederick thought of music that must have stuck him as pretty bizarre, but dedications to major aristocrats were standard practice and the royal acceptance of a composer's dedicatory tribute was a courtesy that could only have been good for sales.

The very first sonata in the set reveals Bach's intention to strike out on new paths. This is the piece with the famous slow movement that incorporates an operatic recitative. After the deliberate, sorrowful introduction, the right hand "speaks" passionately over accompanying chords in the left hand. Bach's innovation here had far-reaching consequences in later music. Haydn knew these sonatas, and we find instrumental recitative featuring in his famous trilogy of symphonies Nos. 6–8 "Le Matin, Le Midi, and Le Soir" (Morning, Noon, and Night). The most famous example of instrumental recitative occurs at the start of the finale of Beethoven's Ninth Symphony. We don't need to be able to prove a direct line of descent to note that all three composers shared a desire to give instrumental music the same sort of expressive specificity as vocal music, and did it in similar ways.

Sonata No. 2 features an especially harmonically daring opening movement, with a deeply affecting minor-key digression toward the end of its first half and a very adventurous development section. The slow central Adagio opens with a hymnlike first theme spiked with arresting dissonances: one of Bach's "timeless" melodies that sounds as though it could have been composed yesterday. The key of E major often has a certain radiant quality perfectly captured in Sonata No. 3's opening Allegro, music that strives to retain the innocent tunefulness of its main theme. In the central Adagio, a lonely theme seems to wander through a landscape alternately desolate and tranquil. Again, notice how the use of unexpected harmony lends the music an extra depth of feeling. The finale is both virtuosic and full-textured, with powerful climaxes.

All of the slow movements in these sonatas are extensively developed, nowhere more so than in Sonata No. 4. The only sonata in this set in a minor key, its outer movements are fast and furious, but the Adagio offers a particularly fine example of how Bach handles a seemingly innocent major-key theme in such a way as to create an emotionally ambiguous, wistful meditation hovering between unruffled serenity and touching pathos. A similar quality characterizes the Andante of Sonata No. 5, a piece that can't seem to decide if it wants to be major or minor. The principal tune of this sonata's finale is particularly memorable. Sonata No. 6 has an opening movement with multiple personalities reflected in rapidly shifting textures and harmonies, and a finale that constantly tries to throw the player off course rhythmically before its surprising, soft close.

"Württemburg" Sonatas, Wq 49 (1744)

No. 1 in A Minor
No. 2 in A-flat Major
No. 3 in E Minor
No. 4 in B-flat Major
No. 5 in E-flat Major
No. 6 in B Minor

Dedicated to Charles Eugene, Duke of Württemberg, the six sonatas of Wq 49 proclaim their bold intentions by the very fact that three of them are rooted in the minor mode. The reason is not just the simplistic concept that sad music should appear as frequently as the happy stuff. Minor keys are, in general, more difficult than major ones on account of the harmonic instability of the minor scale (which has several different forms), and which encourages both a wider range of keys and thus a higher level of affective dissonance. "Harmonic instability" might scare people. Including three such works in a set of six was highly unusual both in Bach's epoch and afterward, and it immediately sets a tone of high seriousness.

The first sonata is one of Bach's biggest. With all of its repeats observed it lasts around seventeen minutes, eight for the first movement alone. Marked "Moderato," the opening movement contains a vast wealth of material leading, after a mostly calm and lyrical Andante, to a very exciting and virtuosic finale. Its development section is particularly intense, the tension building steadily and spilling over into the recapitulation. Sonata No. 2 couldn't represent a larger contrast. It's a gracious and humorous piece that explores the different ways in which Bach can ruffle the feathers of the cheerful emotions that predominate in all three movements. In the initial Un poco allegro and the ensuing Andante, this involves sudden digressions into stern minor keys at strategic points; in the giddy finale Bach tosses in a couple of his characteristically tipsy, rising chromatic scales in the bass.

Bach opens Sonata No. 3 with a rhapsodic introduction in slow tempo before the movement takes off with a nervous, repeated-note theme. This really wonderful piece has as much to do with the extreme contrast between these two ideas as it does any other notion of form. The slow movement takes its simple-sounding opening and extends it in all kinds of unexpected directions, while the finale packs so many surprises of rhythm and harmony into its approximately two minutes' duration that it seems much larger than it really is. In the end, it evaporates mysteriously into nothingness. No. 4's hearty, good-natured first movement leaves us unprepared for the twilit Andante, a winding, eerie melody pierced now and then by sudden shafts of major-key light. The finale is very humorous and eccentric: its main theme is little more than a brief exclamation followed by a squiggle of notes, and you won't believe what follows from that.

E-flat major in later music became the key of heroism, thanks to Beethoven's "Eroica" Symphony and Richard Strauss's epic tone poem *Ein Heldenleben* (A Hero's Life). Bach's opening for Sonata No. 5 seems to anticipate this in its grand gestures, but he underlines the pomposity amusingly with strange harmonies and the occasional unexpected pause. The slow movement pretends to be unflappable in its gentle onward flow, but curious dissonances and trills along the way lead us to question its peaceful intentions. This movement provides an excellent example of how embellishments enrich musical expression beyond serving as mere decoration. The finale is a bouncy, uninhibited romp in a "popular music" rhythm but, this being Bach, a couple of very funny pauses keep us guessing as the movement proceeds.

More stylized vocal declamation, and a harmonic scheme that never resolves in the way it seemingly wants to, feature prominently in the first movement of the Sonata in B Minor. The music's discontinuity is very strange and disconcerting, and the ending in the right key comes as a positive relief—as, for that matter, does the comparative mellifluous normalcy of the major-key Adagio non molto. Is the finale—a baroque two-part invention—a tribute to Bach's father? Perhaps, but its hyperactivity and extravagant keyboard compass might at the same time be poking gentle fun at what for C. P. E. must have been some very challenging keyboard exercises at the time he first encountered them.

Reprisensonaten (Sonatas with Varied Reprises), Wq 50 (1760)

No. 1 in F Major
No. 2 in G Major
No. 3 in A Minor
No. 4 in D Minor
No. 5 in B-flat Major
No. 6 in C Minor

When C. P. E. Bach dedicated this set of six sonatas to the Princess Anna Amalia of Prussia in 1760, he was in a very different position than he had enjoyed in the 1740s. Since publication of the his *Essay on the True Art of Keyboard Playing* in 1753, he had earned recognition as the major German authority on the subject, and his standing in musical circles not just in Berlin but in northern Europe (at least) had never been higher. The *Reprisensonaten* obviously were intended to capitalize on his success not just as a composer of keyboard music generally, but as one with unique pedagogical credentials specifically. For more information on Bach's intentions and the aesthetics of varied reprises, I refer you to the extensive discussion (and accompanying recording) of Sonata No. 6 in C Minor in Chapter 2, "Listening to C. P. E."

One of the outstanding characteristics of these sonatas is the lyrical quality of their quick movements. With the exception of the driving presto opening of No. 3 in A Minor—one of the most exciting pieces in all of Bach—most of these sonatas begin with music in moderate tempo: Allegretto (grazioso) in Nos. 1, 2, and 4, or Poco allegro in No. 5. No. 6, as we have already seen, is a special case, being a set of variations in one movement, but its speed also is a relatively measured march tempo. This means longer themes that offer greater opportunities to vary the reprises, and music that gives the listener time to hear the difference. Because the first movements are already so melodically well developed, most of the slow movements are quite short, and two of them, in Sonatas Nos. 1 and 4, have the feel of transitions or introductions to the finale.

Another strategy that Bach employs to clarify the music's didactic purpose is to incorporate a very catchy rhythmic motive into a theme that more or less retains its shape on repetition. In other words, it does not vary much, other than by key or pitch level, and these rhythmically firm shapes serve as "anchors," letting us know exactly where we are in the otherwise shifting seas of melody. The most telling example of this occurs in the first movement of Sonata No. 2, where the "anchor" is not only a loud, memorable rising phrase with strong accents and repeated notes in the bass, but it also sounds audibly related to the opening theme of the vigorous finale.

The music of these sonatas is as expressively affecting as ever, with Bach paying particular attention to the sequence of feelings that each sonata explores. The placement in tandem of the Sonatas in A Minor and D Minor is particularly revealing in this respect, as they are in many ways mirror images. Sonata No. 3 begins with a furious Presto, the only such first movement in the set. Its main theme sounds suspiciously like a desperate minor-key version of the first Allegro in the Suite in F Major from Handel's *Water Music*. The sonata ends with a wistful Allegro moderato ma innocentemente, a remarkable verbal indication of Bach's intentions. Sonata No. 5 goes in the opposite direction, opening Allegretto grazioso, and concluding with a stern Allegro. Once again, the presence of three sonatas in minor keys attests to Bach's seriousness of purpose as well as the wide range of moods he wishes us to experience.

Sequel of Six Sonatas, Wq 51 (1761)

No. 1 in C Major
No. 2 in B-flat Major
No. 3 in C Minor
No. 4 in D Minor
No. 5 in F Major
No. 6 in G Minor

Bach's *Reprisensonaten* (Sonatas with Varied Reprises) were a big hit. Never one to pass up a good commercial opportunity, he followed them up with two "sequels," additional sets of six sonatas. He was now sitting on a large collection of sonatas that he could draw upon to assemble new collections, mixing freshly composed pieces with works from his inventory.

These are not sonatas with varied reprises, by and large, but they do contain some really splendid formal innovations and imaginative strokes that Bach's audience would have appreciated. First and foremost among them is that fact that the music often plays continuously through multiple movements. In Sonata No. 1 the heroic first movement flows directly into the second, and the insane finale follows with only the briefest of pauses. This last movement does everything that Bach can think of to create his particular brand of organized chaos, with unpredictable pauses, amusing digressions, and the player seeming to forget how the tune goes.

Sonata No. 2 begins with a majestic introduction, Adagio sostenuto, before continuing with a very highly developed Presto. However, at the very end the opening Adagio returns, now "mesto" (sad), and morphs directly into the slow movement—a marvelous conception, beautifully timed and executed. The finale is a gently flowing river of pastoral melody, with a full coda attached to its second half repeat.

The first movement of No. 3 in C Minor uses unexpected silence and harmonic ambiguity to far more serious purpose than does the finale of No. 2. The slow movement is merely a very vocal, declamatory connecting link to the similarly emphatic finale, marked "Allegro ma non tanto." Its main theme recalls that of the first movement in what is, by any standard, a very highly unified piece of writing. The quiet ending is wonderful, and particularly "right" emotionally. Music such as this later would come to be called symphonic as a result of its sense of organic inevitability, even when not written for orchestra.

Sonata No. 4's opening movement is clearly preludial. It lasts less than three minutes, is dominated by its very memorable opening gesture, and seems to end earlier than it needs to, but Bach's intentions become clear in the ensuing Largo sostenuto, a very highly developed movement with another one of those "speaking" introductions. The music hovers throughout between major and minor, displaying poignant melancholy. It comes to a complete close. The finale is the largest movement in the sonata, a mercurial Presto with virtuosic writing in the upper reaches of the keyboard. It's neither sad nor stern: more fantastical in the way that Mendelssohn later would be in such music as the Scherzo from *A Midsummer Night's Dream*.

Varied reprises return in the long (nearly five minutes), pastoral opening movement of Sonata No. 5. It is longer, in fact, than the remaining two movements combined, and it covers a very wide range of expression within its surging and largely uninterrupted rhythmic flow. So dominant is the character of the first movement that the remaining two, both with varied repeats, reveal a similar rhythmic complexion. The first movement is in 6/8, the Larghetto in 3/8, and the finale an Allegro in 3/4, but the continuous triplet patterns makes it feel like 9/8. The result is a unifying pulse—rhythmic groups of three eighth notes—that seems to carry through the entire sonata.

The final sonata, in G minor, has a very harmonically adventurous first movement whose leaping first theme in dotted rhythm reveals itself to be open to just about anything it feels like attempting. Another tiny slow movement ambiguously oscillating between major and minor leads to a concluding Allegretto whose pensive main theme in evenly moving eighth notes makes the music sound like it's running along much more quickly than it really is. A "sequel" this set of sonatas may be, but Bach clearly had no intention of offering just more of the same.

Second Sequel of Six Sonatas, Wq 52 (1763)

No. 1 in E-flat Major
No. 2 in D Minor
No. 3 in G Minor
No. 4 in F-sharp Minor
No. 5 in E Major
No. 6 in E Minor

Bach's next "sequel" offered his public a major serving of musical red meat: four sonatas in minor keys, all with fully developed slow movements, all featuring a healthy dose of keyboard virtuosity. The very first, in E-flat major, opens with a burst of energy and features in its first movement a remarkable development section full of harmonic surprises. Its slow movement, a very slow Adagio assai, has the character of a funeral march, with hesitant dotted rhythms intriguingly similar to those in Beethoven's "Eroica" Symphony. The finale is a whirling perpetual motion piece that flies by as if in a single, astonishing phrase.

Sonata No. 2, in D minor, largely avoids the scarier aspects of that key. The opening movement is a graceful Allegretto, the finale a motoric Allegro with more than a touch of grim humor. The one threatening moment, typically, occurs in the mostly tranquil Larghetto e sempre piano ("slowish and always soft"), which isn't *always* soft, but, in fact, runs into a menacing fortissimo just before the end.

Sonata No. 3 is very unconventional. It accelerates as is goes, but only slightly, from Andante ed amoroso ("lovingly"), to Allegretto, to Allegro moderato. The soulful first movement, with varied reprises, is incomplete, and flows directly into the jaunty, major-key Allegretto march. This movement is so cheerful that its mood and some of its rhythmic figures overflow into the finale, a minuet in all but name, in ABA form. It starts in the major, moving to the home key of G minor only for its B section. The return of A is a varied reprise that leads to a poetic coda, and an ending firmly in the major—a remarkable and very unusual work.

The first movement of Sonata No. 4, in the unusual key of F-sharp minor, is amazing. It alternates two kinds of music: a virtuosic toccata similar in sound to the famous Solfeggio in C Minor (discussed with its recording in Chapter 2, "Listening to C. P. E.") and a tender, major-key melody in what seems to be a slower tempo. Indeed, the entire point of such pieces as the solfeggio is to prepare the player for the kind of writing as we find here. These two ideas battle for tonal supremacy, with F-sharp minor winning in the end and transforming the lyrical theme into something touchingly sad. The development section is huge—so huge that it comes to a full stop, as if to take a breath, before the recapitulation. Played with all of its repeats the movement would last about seven or eight minutes, but the second half is so long that the repeat hardly seems necessary, especially since it's very hard to imagine how the music can be improved by any variations the second time around. It's really just an incredible ride.

The Poco andante slow movement is also quite large and very impressively sustained. Bach even leaves room for an improvised cadenza (preferably a short one) just before the end. Its mood is very contented and songlike. Only a few disturbing moments, including one of Bach's favorite rising chromatic bass lines, hint at darker things under the surface; but this is one sonata in which the story of the first movement, with the minor key triumphant, defines the whole. Like the opening, the finale contrasts two types of music: a jagged motive in dotted rhythm, and evenly rushing eighth notes. It all happens, however, in a much more compressed way. The two ideas alternate rapidly, and sometimes even combine, on the way to a definitive conclusion in the home key. This is a real concert piece, aimed more at the professional performer than the domestic consumer, however gifted and ambitious. The music practically begs for an audience.

After the amplitude and grandeur of the Sonata in F-sharp Minor, Sonata No. 5 impresses as notably more intimate. The opening movement employs a similar toccata-like texture to that of Sonata No. 4, but only the quick bits, without the contrasting lyricism, and, of course, the mood of E major is completely different: brilliant and effervescent. The central Larghetto is truly "inward" in its refined tranquility. Its form is a simple ABA, with Bach leaving any embellishment of the reprise of "A" up to the player. In the finale we return to the allegro tempo of the first movement and music that's all charm and hearty good humor.

Bach closes this set with another "symphonic" piece in three especially well-balanced movements. The initial, moody Allegro is very dramatic and packed with ideas. Most recognizable is a loud outburst in big, resonant chords that call for a very full-toned instrument for their proper effect. Unusually, the Adagio has a nickname: "*L'Einschnitt*." The German word means a "break" or "cut," and in music it can refer to a short motive or rhythmic figure. In this movement, it probably explains the fact that succeeding phrases borrow a bit of the prior ones, but then take the music in a new direction. The result is a kind of gentle dialogue or chain of associations that spins itself out continuously over the course of some three and a half minutes or so.

C. P. E. marks the finale "Allegro di molto." The *di*, by the way, doesn't mean anything. Lots of composers use the designation, but there's no difference between "Allegro di molto" and just plain "Allegro molto." This has been driving me crazy for years, so I finally asked an authority—my brother-in-law, who is Milanese—and he confirmed that *di* is simply jargon or archaic and not part of normative spoken Italian at all. This finale, in any case, is another meaty piece of minor-key angst, with an agitated underlying eighth-note pulse. It opens in midstride, and we don't really feel either the tempo or the key until the first fortissimo breaks in and tells us in no uncertain terms. Haydn learned a lot from "off tonic" openings such as this, and used them often in his symphonies: the first movements of Nos. 86, and 92 "Oxford," for example.

Six Easy Keyboard Sonatas, Wq 53 (1766)

No. 1 in C Major
No. 2 in B-flat Major
No. 3 in A Minor
No. 4 in B Minor
No. 5 in C Major
No. 6 in F Major

What's so easy about these six sonatas? Well, some are quite short. Three of them, the two in C major and the one in A minor, can be played mostly on the white keys, and the left-hand parts may be a bit less tricky than usual. The harmonies aren't as weird as Bach sometimes gets, and he avoids some of the wilder disruptions and incongruities designed to throw both players and listeners for a loop. Otherwise, these are lovely works, and as if to make up for their normalcy, Bach has filled them with an extra fund of genuinely attractive melody. The "easy" part applies not just to the technique, but also to their approachability. He also designates the movements to be played "tenderly," a very unusual marking at any time in musical history. Another is "grazioso," and the very first sonata opens with Allegretto ed arioso: in other words, in the manner of a song.

Of course, this being Bach, it's a very elaborate and abundantly decorated song, with much of the essential ornamentation written out. This certainly makes it easy to know *what* to play, but actually to play it? Not so much. Even here, we must be careful to distinguish between a simpler style, which this may be, and music for true beginners, which these pieces certainly are not. Sonata No. 1 also has an extraordinary middle movement, the Andantino, con tenerezza (with tenderness). Its form is ABABA, plus a coda based on "B." In other words, it's basically a rondo, and the "B" episode is a march with a very memorable refrain that you will swear you've heard somewhere before. The finale is a whirlwind Presto, quite short, but still calling for considerable digital dexterity.

Sonata No. 2 is a short work, with an opening Allegretto grazioso that really is "gracious," but also melodically very beautiful. You may want to play it over again right away. The brief, minor-key Larghetto that follows tosses in a few spicy dissonances to enhance the pathos. Bach asks that the finale be played Allegro ma non presto, but it still moves very quickly, in continuous sixteenth notes. Listen to the left hand. This is where the melody really is. Both here and in Sonata No. 1, the finale should follow the slow movement without a break. In No. 3, however, the Poco andante follows the initial Allegro without pause. This is a very characteristic sonata, from its grim opening to the hymn-like solemnity, with minor-key shadings, of the slow movement. Only its brevity perhaps gives it away as "easy," but the finale is a virtuoso movement in which Bach pulls no punches.

He turns up the heat still more for Sonata No. 4 in B Minor. Although marked "Allegretto," the first movement has a busy texture built out of innumerable repetitions of a tiny, four-note motive. The first part also tosses in a nice harmonic curve ball that Bach exploits to surprising effect in the recapitulation. All three movements in this work should be played continuously. The Largo e tenero is the second "tender" piece in the set, while the Presto finale whirls along in steady triplets, with even the left hand having plenty to contribute to the music's driving rhythmic motion. Only the central development section reveals a few moments of hesitation.

We're back in C major for Sonata No. 5, and a first movement that gushes melody in a steady stream. The minor-key Poco adagio is quite short, less than two minutes, but full of feeling, with a shocking non-ending when the finale erupts out of nowhere in the same minor key—but only for a moment. The music suddenly remembers that it's in three-quarter time and starts to waltz away in the major like a barrel organ tune at a carnival. The joy doesn't last however; the recapitulation recasts everything squarely in the movement's original minor key and what started out in a sunny C major ends emphatically in distress. Bach's point in including two sonatas nominally in the same "easy" key couldn't be clearer. Technical simplicity in no way limits the music's expressive intensity, or Bach's creative imagination.

Bach throws caution to the breeze in Sonata No. 6, an extraordinary work in which, once again, all three movements are played continuously. The extremely athletic Allegro di molto first movement, with varied repeats, features a marvelous, fully composed transition to an Andantino full of biting dissonance and sudden chordal outbursts. If you were listening carefully you might have noticed some very similar dissonant passages in the first movement. Again, the slow movement isn't complete but leads directly into the final Presto, where Bach combines the soulful mood of the Andantino with the first movement's aggressive eagerness. In case you were wondering, the Andantino wins; the final bars are the very epitome of sly humor. By the time average home keyboardists got through these sonatas, they certainly would be "ready for their close-up," as the saying goes.

Sonatas for Ladies, Wq 54 (1770)

No. 1 in F Major
No. 2 in C Major
No. 3 in D Minor
No. 4 in B-flat Major
No. 5 in D Major
No. 6 in A Major

This is Bach's lightest set of keyboard sonatas. They are mostly quite short, with especially brief slow movements, and only one in a minor key. However, as with the "easy" sonatas, it would be a mistake to think that Bach was dumbing down his style. "Adapting" it would be the better term. The existence of these sonatas points to a genuine sociological phenomenon: the arrival of women as a commercial force in the world of music. Naturally there have always been female professional musicians, especially singers, and the wealthy were expected to sing, dance, and play a musical instrument. Bach certainly knew several lady virtuosos: women with the chops for a major career but who, for reasons of propriety, mostly kept to their salons, or performed publically only occasionally. Sarah Levy, who commissioned Bach's final concerto, was one such (so were her sisters), and he never felt that he needed to make any allowance for her sex—at least that we know of.

The keyboard became the female instrument of choice, at least partly, because it could be played without an unacceptable loss of womanly grace and poise. Woodwind instruments involved a most unacceptable puckering of the lips, moistening of reeds, and other very unladylike facial contortions. Brass and percussion players still belonged to the military. The violin was, obviously, a soprano instrument and thus a dubious proposition for upstanding, heterosexual women until well into the Victorian period. As for the cello—the very thought of a woman sitting in the necessary spread-legged playing position was simply unthinkable. So, keyboards it was.

These sonatas were written before Bach moved to Hamburg, in 1765/6, but he only published them in 1770. It is not unreasonable to assume that by this time he was aware of a hitherto untapped domestic market among the musically literate women of the burgeoning middle classes, and he put this collection together to take advantage of it. In my opinion, his strategy was not to select music that was short or easy because his target consumer was female; rather, he had to find music for an audience new to his style entirely, and who were getting to know him from scratch. Thus, the "easy" sonatas are Bach (slightly) simplified, for those who may know him but fear his difficulty. The "lady" sonatas are Bach for the entirely uninitiated—people who may have known him by reputation but not through his actual works.

The very first sonata, in F major, lends a certain level of credence to this theory. Simple sonatas in two movements were common during the rococo period, including many by Bach's brother J. C. (check out Johann Christian's set of sonatas, Op. 17 for several examples). Open this particular two-movement package, however, and inside we find vintage C. P. E. Not only does the first movement contain its share of unusual harmonies and sudden surprises; it gradually morphs into an actual slow movement, coming to a quiet close. The second movement, too, while short, features varied repeats and some very rhythmically tricky figuration all the way through. So, here is Bach announcing himself to a new audience, accommodating what he takes to be their needs without dumbing down his style. The packaging looks slightly different, but the contents are the real deal.

Sonata No. 2 features a fully developed first movement containing a rich variety of themes and motives, moving in typically unpredictable directions. The slow movement is an elegiac set of mini-variations less than a minute long: three versions of the same six-bar idea. For his finale, Bach offers a boisterous Allegro with plenty of harmonic and rhythmic variety. Sonata No. 3 has a big first movement over which he took great care, marking dynamic gradations often from one note to the next. It maintains its initial dark character throughout, rarely straying away from minor keys. The Larghetto slow movement has two halves, both repeated, with some striking dissonances in the second half adding a bittersweet flavor. Although short, the concluding Prestissimo proves that it's possible to be humorous in a minor key even when the main theme is little more than a rising scale.

Sonata No. 4 is the tiniest of the set, barely five minutes long, with all repeats varied (or no repeats, if that makes more sense). It's too short to develop a great deal of expressive depth, but the outer movements are good, clean fun and the central Andante siciliano is a beautiful slow dance of haunting melancholy.

The next work in the set is back to full size. Its first movement has a particularly substantial development section that sounds as if it wants to be cheerful, but the mood darkens as it proceeds. The following Andante, too, has a strongly pathetic character, its sadness enhanced by the occasional clashing note thrown into the mix. For a work in D major, the finale has a curiously ambivalent feel—call it a serious if still contented basic demeanor. It's a big movement, almost exactly as long as the first but with varied repeats, which make it sound even larger than it really is.

The concluding Sonata in A Major is a particularly wonderful piece, with a clearly introductory opening movement starting with a bizarre theme whose dynamic extremes and quirky rhythm give no hint of the fact that it's really a waltz—although technically waltzes hadn't been invented yet. We only discover this when the music turns decisively to the minor, a place it seemingly wants to stay. There's something very modern sounding about this music, its humor as much as its sexy swagger. The movement, in simple ABABA form, doesn't end. Instead, the opening idea transitions to the Larghetto, a very harmonically sophisticated two minutes of song. Like the opening, it seems not to know whether it wants to be major or minor, but it leans toward the latter. The finale, a warmly enthusiastic Allegretto in flowing rhythm and the longest movement in the sonata, makes the ultimate decision. It opts decisively for the home key of A major.

Six Keyboard Sonatas for Connoisseurs and Amateurs, First Volume, Wq 55 (1779)

No. 1 in C Major (1773)
No. 2 in F Major (1758)
No. 3 in B Minor (1774)
No. 4 in A Major (1765)
No. 5 in F Major (1772)
No. 6 in G Major (1765)

Bach's last six published collections of keyboard music were aptly named. The *Kenner und Liebhaber* (Connoisseurs and Amateurs) series contains the largest and most varied assortment of pieces in extended forms that he ever assembled for the music consumer. Critics and scholars have debated for generations just which works were intended for connoisseurs and which for amateurs, but I tend to take the view that the word *und* in the title means what is says, and that everything in these collections is for everyone.

As you can see from the dates listed next to each piece in this group, Bach did not compose this music to order. He drew upon his already existing stock of unpublished sonatas and assembled them as a set. The ordering of the individual items was very carefully done. Sonatas 1, 3, and 5 are all relatively brief; Nos. 2, 4, and 6 rank with the largest that Bach ever wrote, lasting some fifteen-plus minutes each, depending on tempo and the performer's handling of repeats. This single work in a minor key, the Sonata in B Minor, is placed toward the center, but you shouldn't think that the relative dearth of minor key signals any lack of seriousness or emotional depth.

As we have seen, most sonatas in major keys will include a central slow movement in the minor; but more significantly, it's an interesting fact with many composers that their mature work contains a wider harmonic range more generally, and the degree of contrast is most evident in pieces that at least begin in major keys. This is very true of late Haydn, and we find the same principle at work in C. P. E. Bach. There's a new fluidity of movement in this music that's very evident even on a casual listen, and it's one of the factors that permits Bach to include pieces written on a much larger scale than usual. In the later sets, as you will hear, this broader vision also characterizes the rondos and fantasias, and enable him to give them his personal stamp.

This set begins, like J. S. Bach's *Well-Tempered Clavier*, with an arpeggio prelude in C major. Bach senior's precedes a fugue, but this one turns out to be the first movement of a sonata. The Andante, in a minor key, has a marked Slavic quality in its opening gesture, almost like one of Dvorák's slower Slavonic Dances or Dumka movements, while the finale is a gawky, humorous Allegretto that seems at times to approach Prokofiev in its "wrong note" classicism. Accordingly to contemporary sources, the F Major Sonata was one of Bach's favorites. It is clavichord music, since it contains notation for the kind of vibrato that was only possible on that instrument. If you have a recording featuring the clavichord, pay attention to the passage about a minute in (and whenever it returns later), featuring repeated notes in the right hand, accompanied by dotted rhythms in the left. It's a subtle effect (or it should be), but usually audible to some degree.

The first movement has no ending. Instead, Bach composes a transition (also with vibrato) leading to the very beautiful, flowing, minor-key Larghetto. This is a very sad and songful piece, and here the music at last achieves closure. The finale starts off with what sounds like a rollicking popular song, but there's a big development section that covers a very wide harmonic range before stumbling into the highly varied recapitulation. All in all, this sonata offers a good sense of Bach's expanded scope. Significantly it's the earliest piece in the collection, but it's one he kept to himself for at least two decades before publishing it here.

Continuity also marks the B Minor Sonata, which begins as though already in progress. Its three short movements all share a similar moderate tempo, while the Andante and concluding Cantabile flow together; so the entire work, which only lasts about seven minutes, feels like a strongly unified whole. Bach drives the point home by remaining in a minor key for most of what is technically the central slow movement.

Another very large work follows. The first movement of the A Major Sonata lasts as long as the entire previous *work*. It's a very fast, athletic piece that requires a big-toned instrument for the proper effect. Despite its frenetic energy, once again Bach composes a slow transition to the minor-key slow movement, at the end of which he leaves room for an improvised cadenza. The finale is very quirky, with odd stops and starts and some very arresting repeated-note effects. Almost as long as the first movement, it completes a work composed on the grandest possible scale.

Bach already offered a very large Sonata in F Major; his second in that key is one of the smaller ones, but it's no less rewarding musically. Just listen to that opening—you'd think this will be another minor-key piece, but after some hesitation the music arrives at the major mode, as advertised. Even here, though, the themes have a curiously unsettled quality (the E-flat in the main tune's second phrase is definitely weird). If this opening movement feels "unsettled," then the Adagio mesto is just plain disturbed. Although brief, Bach's harmony has seldom sounded freer or more anguished, while the equally pithy finale just barely manages to snatch F major victor from jaws of, well, if not defeat, then *otherness*.

The first movement of the large G Major Sonata is very rhapsodic, and liberally sprinkled with the kind of writing we will hear in Bach's fantasias—numerous short and highly varied gestures that hardly can be called tunes in the normative sense. This same observation also characterizes the Andante, which starts with an ethereal introductory descending line, and proceeds in flowing sixteenth-note arabesques that now and then come together to suggest a melody before moving on. Although marked "Allegro di molto," the finale is written so that its principal idea sounds deliberately nonchalant. There's a battle brewing, between fast and slow, loud and soft, and in the development section the wild scales once again foreshadow Prokofiev (the second subject of the finale in the Third Piano Concerto). Over one passage Bach writes the word "emphatic." He seems to have saved his most original piece for last.

Sonatas and Rondos for Fortepiano, for Connoisseurs and Amateurs, Second Volume, Wq 56 (1780)

Rondo No. 1 in C Major (Wq 56/1)
Sonata No. 1 in G Major (Wq 56/2)
Rondo No. 2 in D Major (Wq 56/3)
Sonata No. 2 in F Major (Wq 56/4)
Rondo No. 3 in A Minor (Wq 56/5)
Sonata No. 3 in A Major (Wq 56/6)

Bach promised his publisher Breitkopf (still one of the major German music publishers today) that the second volume in the *Kenner und Liebhaber* series would be completely different from its predecessor, and he wasn't kidding. Here we find him launching his rondos for keyboard, and this is also the first collection of pieces in which Bach lists the fortepiano specifically as the instrument of choice. It thus represents a signal historical moment in the evolution of music for keyboards. As in the previous set, there is only one work in a minor key, but here and in the next two volumes, he takes pains to pair a rondo with a sonata in the same key, but the opposite mode (major vs. minor). Just why he did this, or what significance it may have had other than to explore the expressive boundaries of specific keys, is anyone's guess.

The rondos can be considered as a group. If you're familiar with the Viennese classical rondo, usually a perky finale in ABACA form, these pieces may come as something of a shock. As already discussed in my introduction to the keyboard music, Bach's rondos usually have many more sections, and they often begin with a placid theme in moderate tempo, the better to offset the music of the numerous short episodes. Also, he had no compunction against writing sad or turbulent pieces in minor keys, including this Rondo in A Minor, belying the form's reputation as something light and easy.

The three sonatas, all relatively short, also share a certain family resemblance in that they explore different ways of combining movements into a larger whole, but otherwise couldn't be more different. The G Major Sonata has three full movements that are all linked together. Bach uses the finale to do just about everything he can think of with a rapid, descending scale. The F Major Sonata has only two brief movements, about two and half minutes each, but these are also joined. The opening Andantino moves from major to minor, only to be strongly contradicted by the Presto finale. Finally, the A Major Sonata compresses the three normal movements into one, simply marked "Allegretto." Any changes in pace are written into the music, with the central slow movement reduced to a connecting link just a few bars long.

Bach told his publisher that he expected this last piece to be played throughout at the same speed, with all repeats observed. If this is done the form takes care of itself and the three-in-one structure comes across with perfect clarity. Although the works in this set are less complex and technically challenging than those in the first collection, once again he demonstrates, as he did in the keyboard concertos Wq 43, that the challenge of doing something "easy" often goes hand in hand with striking formal innovations.

Finally, note the naming conventions within these mixed sets. As far as Wotquenne is concerned, the pieces are simply numbered 1 through 6, as I have indicated; but Bach (who obviously knew nothing about Wotquenne) numbered the individual works by genre: Rondo 1,

Rondo 2, Sonata 1, Sonata 2, and so on. It's not likely that any confusion will arise, but you should just be aware of it.

Sonatas and Rondos for Fortepiano, for Connoisseurs and Amateurs, Third Volume, Wq 57 (1781)

Rondo No. 1 in E Major
Sonata No. 2 in A Minor
Rondo No. 2 in G Major
Sonata No. 2 in D Minor
Rondo No. 3 in F Major
6. Sonata No. 3 in F Minor

In this third volume, all of the sonatas are full size and take the minor mode, while all of the rondos are in the major. The E Major Rondo is one of Bach's largest and most richly varied, while the G Major is the shortest, with a ritornello theme of unassuming innocence and charm—although it grows up over the course of the piece. The F Major Rondo's quick tempo and witty byplay bring it close to the better-known, Viennese models, although it still contains plenty of typically Bachian personality and surprise as well as his tendency to avoid literal repetition.

The Sonata in F Minor is included in the listening samples with this book, and has already been discussed in detail. No. 2 in A Minor shares with it the fact that the slow movement runs into the finale without a break, but the music itself offers another example of Bach's ability to write in minor keys with humor—note especially his witty use of silence. The entire sonata has a very agitated, even "twitchy" quality that's far from tragic, but still distinctly intense all the same. The slow movement too is very harmonically unpredictable, an observation that applies to the companion D Minor Sonata in general. This piece stays in the minor for the pensive central Cantabile e mesto, and has a very short finale that sounds oddly unresolved at the close. Bach composed this sonata much earlier (1766) but apparently withheld it for a couple of decades, either because he wished to keep it for his own use or because its language was considered too radical to garner much public favor at the time that it was written.

Sonatas, Free Fantasias, and Rondos for Fortepiano, for Connoisseurs and Amateurs, Fourth Volume, Wq 58 (1783)

Rondo No. 1 in A Major
Sonata No. 2 in G Major
Rondo No. 2 in E Major
Sonata No. 2 in E Minor
Rondo No. 3 in B-flat Major
Fantasia No. 1 in E-flat Major
Fantasia No. 2 in A Major

Volume Four in this series introduces a new formal type: the fantasia. We have already discussed Bach's independent Fantasia in F-sharp Minor, Wq 67, so you have an idea of what to expect. Both of the fantasias here have a sort of enlarged ABA form. The "A" sections consist of fast runs, arpeggios, and sequences that gradually take on a more melodic shape. Much of the music has no bar lines and requires great rhythmic freedom from the performer. "B" is a slower interlude, in the case of the E-flat Major Fantasia with very moody chromatic harmony. Bach included these works "to show what a fantast I was," and we can only be thankful that he did. The fantasias constitute the written record of one of the greatest keyboard improvisers before the jazz age.

This is the only set of pieces in the *Kenner und Liebhaber* series to include seven pieces, and three of them are rondos. Bach's contributions to the form were turning out to be very popular. No. 3 in B-flat Major has already been discussed and is included in the listening samples. The other two belong to the type with a more leisurely ritornello theme; that of the A Major Rondo is particularly memorable. It's a pastoral siciliano of great sensitivity and sweetness.

There are only two sonatas in this set. The G major work is very short, about five minutes long, but with varied repeats. Its centerpiece is the second movement, Larghetto e sostenuto—music of great pathos.

The opening Grazioso and concluding Allegretto gently frame the sonata's emotional core. The E Minor Sonata is a much larger piece, about twelve minutes long, whose shape is the mirror image of the G major: two big outer movements full of disquiet enfolding a short, songful Andantino. Although the tempo of the opening movement is only Allegretto, the rhythms become trickier as the music proceeds.

Sonatas, Free Fantasias, and Rondos for Fortepiano, for Connoisseurs and Amateurs, Fifth Volume, Wq 59 (1785)

Sonata No. 1 in E Minor
Rondo No. 1 in G Major
Sonata No. 2 in B-flat Major
Rondo No. 2 in C Minor
Fantasia No. 1 in F Major
6. Fantasia No. 2 in C Major

If you enjoyed the Sonata in F Minor, Wq 57/6, on the track listing, then you will doubtless also like the Sonata in E Minor in this set. Although considerably shorter (about half as long), it has a very similar shape: a driving Presto opening, and a songful Adagio leading to a pathetic Andantino conclusion. But there are also differences. Bach writes a long and very effective transition from the first movement to the Adagio. That movement is extremely brief—really just a connecting link to a finale with varied repeats. The ending is somewhat shocking: the music stops, seemingly in midphrase.

The Sonata in B-flat Major is another one of the big ones, around fifteen minutes long, and full of spirit. Although only marked "Poco allegro," the first movement goes at quite a clip owing to the short note values. At the end of the first part, you might think the soloist is playing "Chopsticks." The central Largo is also a big movement, more than five minutes long, and surprisingly in a major key, but with a high quota of wonderfully effective and affecting dissonance to give the melody extra poignancy. After such an intense slow movement Bach lets his hair down in the concluding Andantino grazioso, music of great charm and easy humor.

The two rondos in this set are very highly contrasted. That in G major is one of Bach's biggest, and spends a lot of time in minor keys. It requires a high degree of virtuosity from the player. The C minor one opens humorously with a tune that can't seem to remember how it's supposed to go. You can't miss it whenever it returns, and the minor key here seems to represent not so much sorrow as it does sheer panic at not knowing the tune. Bach has a blast varying this memory lapse on its repeated returns, and you will definitely have an equal amount of fun listening. I won't spoil the story by giving away how it ends.

In keeping with the concept, fantasias can and do vary widely from one another. That in F major starts with the familiar free passage sporting scales and other virtuoso gestures, then it settles down to an extended melodic episode leading to a brief return of the opening; then a new episode, prestissimo, leads to yet another reprise (heavily varied) of the beginning by way of conclusion. In other words, the form is basically that of a rondo: ABACA. The C Major Fantasia is another of the more extended ones, with a humorous motive to lead off and lots of different sections in tempos ranging from prestissimo to andantino to allegretto. Once again the frequent return of the initial motive between episodes gives the piece a strong rondo feel.

Sonata in C Minor, Wq 60 (1785)

Published all by itself, this tiny sonata less than five minutes long makes an impact out of all proportion to its actual dimensions. The opening Allegretto really stresses the "minor" in the home key. It is music of genuine anguish, while the slow movement, only about half a minute in total, remains committed to the minor key as well. The finale interrupts with an outburst of petulance that a couple of detours to more cheerful modes can't assuage. This is a Chihuahua among the sonatas: small but fierce.

Sonatas, Free Fantasias, and Rondos for Fortepiano for Connoisseurs and Amateurs, Sixth Volume, Wq 61 (1787)

Rondo No. 1 in E-flat Major
Sonata No. 1 in D Major
Fantasia No. 1 in B-flat Major
Rondo No. 2 in D Minor
Sonata No. 2 in E Major
6. Fantasia No. 2 in C Major

The later volumes in this series sold less well than the earlier ones, perhaps a case of market saturation. It's always important to keep in mind, when we talk about "the public" and "popularity," that the true audience for art music has always been relatively small. A large print run for Bach consisted of about a thousand copies—that's all—and the entire population of Hamburg around 1800 was only approximately 130,000. Even Bach's carefully cultivated network of agents and foreign sales representatives usually took copies of new publications in the tens, not the dozens or hundreds. So, there's very little to be learned about reception from mere sales statistics. Certainly the actual content of this last major volume of keyboard music published in Bach's lifetime maintains the same high standard as the rest.

As you can see, these pieces are organized in two sets, each containing a rondo, a sonata, and a fantasia. The first rondo starts with a mellow theme undermined by an uncooperative bass line. As the music proceeds, that bass line becomes increasingly aggressive, with accordingly disruptive results. The tiny D Major Sonata contains mostly quick music, but as always with Bach, even in miniature the music packs a big punch for its size. The best descriptive term for the first movement is *pointillist*. It's a very eccentric piece full of rhythmic tricks and cheerful surprises. As mentioned, many of these very brief sonatas often contain movements that play without pause, and this one is no exception. Bach composes an effective transition to the central Allegretto, a calm interlude only about a minute long, before the frantic finale, Presto di molto, closes the sonata in madcap high spirits. The Fantasia in B-flat is very rich in vividly contrasting ideas that come and go with appropriately improvisational freedom. There's really nothing else to be said for it; you've got to listen and let it do its thing.

The second rondo, in D minor, is one of Bach's quickest in terms of tempo. Because the principal theme is so energetic the episodes, unless actually derived from it, tend to be more relaxed, until matters get more hyper toward the end. Sonata No. 2 in E Minor, is also relatively short, and like its D major companion it contains outer movements in the same tempo (allegretto this time), with all three meant to be played continuously. The first movement is quite short, with a very striking, rising chromatic phrase at the end of each part. Although it does end firmly, the serene Andante follows immediately and flows into a concluding Allegretto with varied repeats, back in the minor. This movement is another "type" we have encountered before, especially in the Sonata in F Minor, Wq 57/6: a lyrical conclusion rich in pathos to a sonata in a minor key.

The set concludes, in the highest of spirits, with the Fantasia in C Major. Its opening idea, Presto di molto, is a very funny gesture featuring repeated notes that can't seem to make up its mind how it's supposed to go. This alternates, rondolike, with episodes of a more serious nature, but humor wins out in the end. There's something very satisfying in hearing Bach wind down his career at the keyboard, as Verdi did in *Falstaff*, with a laugh and (in the final bars) a wise and gentle smile. For a composer whose reputation rests largely on his expression of "negative" emotions, such as sadness, anger, or despair, it seems the ultimate irony.

Keyboard Sonatas Published Individually in Various Volumes, Wq 62

Sonata in B-flat Major, Wq 62/1 (1731, rev. 1744)
Sonata in D Minor, Wq 62/4 (1744)
Sonata in F Minor, Wq 62/6 (1744)
Sonata in C Major, Wq 62/7 (1744)
Sonata in D Minor, Wq 62/15 (1756)
Sonata in G Major, Wq 62/19 (1757)

Twenty-four Bach sonatas were published singly, often in collections or anthologies that included works by other composers. Wotquenne gathered them up under a single numerical designation, and so we have Wq 62, a big hunk of music that's impossible to consider in detail here. Instead, I have created a standard-size "sampler" collection of six sonatas that I found unusually interesting. This is a purely personal selection, of course, and it was not an easy one to make; the rest you can explore as you choose, since virtually every sonata that Bach wrote offers something distinctive and worth hearing.

The Sonata in B-flat Major, Wq 62/1, is Bach's first work in the form, composed when he was just seventeen. Not surprisingly, the outer movements sound a lot like his father, although the counterpoint is much less strict and the music, especially in the finale, has a hyperactive energy and takes a few unexpected turns that could only be C. P. E. The central Andante, a sorrowful minor-key melody spiced with touches of chromaticism, already seems quite characteristic.

For Bach, 1744 was a banner year. Not only did he revise much of his work of the previous decades, but having just published the "Prussian" and "Württemburg" Sonatas, he wrote a bunch of new ones as well. The Wq 62/4 remains in minor keys throughout. Its slow movement is very sad, and very beautiful, with passionate dissonances adding to its emotionality. The outer movements are large and richly developed, with the composer making very effective use of unexpected silences in the finale. This is a very grand and impressive sonata.

I included Wq 62/6 in F Minor principally for its finale. The whole piece is well worth your attention, but the last movement features a remarkable theme marked "Presto spirituoso e staccato" (very fast, witty and detached). There is, incidentally, no difference between *spirituoso* and *spiritoso*, but the rhythm of this idea is exactly the same as the famous "bicycle" music that accompanies Miss Gulch to Dorothy's house to nab Toto in *The Wizard of Oz*. This rhythm dominates the entire movement, and it's just as catchy as in the film, even though the actual melody is somewhat different. Hearing it in this context comes as a bit of a shock.

The Sonata in C Major, Wq 62/7, is the last of the three originally composed in 1744 that I included in this set. It's very much a major-key version of the D Minor Sonata: two big outer movements offset a briefer but still very distinctive central slow movement. The opening shows what Bach can do with themes based on repeated notes, while the Andantino opens with a very powerful gesture in thick, sharp chords. Everything else follows from this simple idea. Although not terribly long in absolute terms (the entire piece plays for about eleven minutes), like the D minor work, this sonata reveals an impressively large scale and range of expression.

Another Sonata in D Minor, Wq 62/15, shows just how different Bach can sound while working in the same key. A short, intimate piece, the music barely touches on its home key before turning to the major. The result is touchingly pathetic, but not stormy or tragic. A soothing Larghetto, very vocal in feel, leads to an agitated finale with some very striking syncopation thrown in for good measure. The last sonata in this selection, Wq 62/19 in G Major, features three well-balanced parts of similar length—around three minutes each. Its outer movements are both very quick, with rapidly varying textures and quirky turns of phrase. The central Andante, in contrast, is very dark, even spooky, with a steady and ominous tread.

One last note before leaving Wq 62: this collection also includes one of Bach's few keyboard pieces in the old baroque style: the Suite in E Minor, Wq 62/12. There's another one in the same key in Wq 65 (No. 4). This one has five movements: Allemande, Courante, Sarabande, Menuet, and Gigue, all except the Menuet being the standard set of dances usually included in works of this type. It's a typically energetic effort, obviously without quite the same degree of personality that we find in the sonatas. Written in 1751, the year following the death of J.

S. Bach, it's a useful reminder that the baroque style was still very much alive when C. P. E. began exploring new paths.

Six Sonatas for the *Essay on the True Method of Keyboard Playing*; with Six New Sonatinas (practice pieces), Wq 63 (1753/86)

SONATAS

No. 1 in C Major

Allegretto tranquillemente

Andante ma innocentemente

Tempo di minuetto con tenerezza

No. 2 D Minor

Allegro con spirito

Adagio sostenuto

Presto

No. 3 A Major

Poco allegro ma cantabile

Andante lusingando

Allegro

No. 4 B Minor

Allegretto grazioso

Largo maestoso

Allegro siciliano e scherzando

No. 5 E-flat Major

Allegro di molto

Adagio assai mesto e sostenuto

Allegretto arioso ed amoroso

No. 6 F Minor

Allegro di molto

Adagio affetuoso e sostenuto

Fantasia

SONATINAS

No. 1 in G Major (Wq 63/7)
No. 2 in E Major (Wq 63/8)
No. 3 in D Major (Wq 63/9)
No. 4 in B-flat Major (Wq 63/10)
No. 5 in F Major (Wq 63/11)
No. 6 in D Minor (Wq 63/12)

In connection with the first part of his *Essay on the True Art of Keyboard Playing*, Bach wrote eighteen *Probestücke* (practice pieces) that he arranged in the form of six sonatas. These were published separately. For pedagogical purposes, he added fingerings and indications for all of the necessary ornaments, including the vibrato that reveals the clavichord as the instrument of choice in at least some of this music (the slow movement of Sonata No. 4 and the concluding Fantasia of Sonata No. 6). Each movement is written in a different key, which means that no sonata ends in the same tonality in which it began, but these are, in all other respects, typical of C. P. E., and even the easiest pieces reveal plenty of his distinctive personality.

Rather than discuss each work in detail, I suggest you have a look at the movement designations, which are unusually specific. Clearly Bach wished to tell the student exactly which affects the music (and presumably the correct performance of it) should evoke. The first sonata alone should be played tranquilly, innocently, and lastly, tenderly. The first movement of the Second Sonata, even though in D minor, is "witty;" that of the Third Sonata is "songful" and its slow movement should be "lusingando" ("flattering"—I have never understood how a performer is supposed to do that; however, another meaning is "alluring," which makes more sense). The finale of the Fourth Sonata is a "joking siciliano," while the Fifth Sonata has a "very said and sustained" Adagio and a finale that is both "singing" and "loving." One of Bach's greatest and moodiest fantasias concludes the Sixth Sonata, preceded by an Adagio that is "affecting and sustained." The Fantasia is the piece that was considered so vocally specific that a colleague of the composer's added words to it from Shakespeare (*Hamlet*) and Socrates. In short, the point about what the music expresses couldn't be made more clearly.

That said, these pieces seem to have proved too difficult for beginners (they really are). Perhaps Bach was more concerned with covering the range of emotions he wanted players to express than with assuring technical facility; and so in 1786, at the very end of his life, he wrote six additional pieces that he called sonatinas—the third time he used that designation, in each case for something very different. These pieces are short, single movements lasting from about one to less than three minutes apiece. They are charming, perfectly suited to their purpose, and the concluding D minor Presto is quite exciting. Of course they are not major Bach, but recordings of the six original sonatas may include them for the sake of completeness.

Six Keyboard Sonatinas, Wq 64 (1734, rev. 1744)

No. 1 in G Major
No. 2 in G Major
No. 3 in A Minor
No. 4 in E Minor
No. 5 in D Major
No. 6 in C Minor

The six early keyboard sonatinas are little gems. Each has three movements lasting about five or six minutes in total. They are thus as long as some full-fledged sonatas. Composed in 1734, when Bach was twenty, they are wholly characteristic of his budding genius. He revised them in 1744, and happily in several cases we know exactly what he did to them. This offers some unique insights into his aesthetic priorities The First Sonatina, for example, originally remained in major keys for all three movements, but in 1744 he replaced the initial Andante with a passionate minor-key movement in the same tempo.

In the Second Sonatina, also in G major, Bach did exactly the same thing as in the First, only in this case a new Largo takes the same music as the original Adagio non molto and converts it from major to minor. The Third Sonatina in A Minor is a remarkably hard-hitting work given its ostensibly "light" character, and Bach seems to have been pretty happy with it as it stood. He revised the Fourth Sonatina in a manner very similar to what he did in the second one, only because the work is in E minor and the original Largo also began in the minor, he recast the same music in the major and added a healthy dollop of pathetic chromaticism as well.

The outer movements of the Fifth Sonatina, in D major, are supple, skittish, and thematically related at the outset, while the central Andantino un poco is very operatic. Once again, in the Sixth Sonatina in C Minor, we find Bach removing a similarly minor-key slow movement and replacing it with an entirely new one in the major. In every single case Bach's revisions increase the music variety, contrast, and range of expression. It would be hard to imagine a more delightful means of learning about Bach's compositional method.

Complete Volume of All Unpublished Keyboard Sonatas, Wq 65

At some point, our good friend Alfred Wotquenne must have just thrown up his hands and decided to pack all of Bach's unpublished sonatas into a single huge group. There are fifty individual works in Wq 65, and as with Wq 62, where we have "only" twenty-four, that is unfortunately far too many to enable discussion of each one individually. We could do it with the fifty-two concertos because there weren't another hundred or so waiting in the wings; but this chapter is already very long and we still want to consider however briefly the remaining pieces, including many that are not sonatas. The size of this collection, alongside the fact that none of these works was published during Bach's lifetime, means that most of them remain as good as unknown. This is a terrible pity. They include some of his largest, boldest, and most original creations, works he clearly reserved for himself or feared to publish on account of their radicalism and daring.

As with Wq 62, to give you a taste of this extraordinary musical treasure trove, I have made what I hope you will agree is a generous selection. I have chosen the following three groups from Wq 65, each containing six sonatas, falling roughly into Bach's early, middle, and late periods; and so they cover his entire career. They reveal his inexhaustible creativity with particular vividness. This music, virtually all of it, is simply amazing.

Group I

Sonata in F Major, Wq 65/1 (1731, rev. 1744)
Sonata in D Minor, Wq 65/3 (1732, rev. 1744)
Sonata in E Minor, Wq 65/5 (1735, rev. 1744)
Sonata in E-flat Major, Wq 65/7 (1736, rev. 1744)
Sonata in G Minor, Wq 65/11 (1739)
Sonata in B Minor, Wq 65/13 (1743)

If the Sonata in B-flat Major, Wq 62/1, was Bach's first sonata, then the Sonata in F Major, Wq 65/1, was the second. It couldn't appear more different. The very opening idea is one of those curiously gawky tunes that sounds more like modern neoclassicism than the late baroque. A wistful, minor-key Andante leads to a humorous finale that begins more like P. D. Q. Bach than it does J. S. After a few frantic baroque gestures, Bach essentially says, "The hell with it," and tries to proceed with a normal melody over a simple accompaniment, but "baroque-isms" keep breaking in.

The opening Allegro di molto of the Sonata in D Minor, Wq 65/3, features a harmonic waywardness that's truly alarming—and a great deal of fun to listen to. Bach compensates for the disturbance, though, in the lyrically exquisite Andante, which is really the heart of the work. The very quick finale drives the sonata home in a rollicking 6/8 meter. In the next sonata, Wq 65/5, the minor mode dominates all three movements. After an elegant opening Allegro, the composer offers a very Italianate siciliano and a finale with an incredibly distinctive principal theme—sort of a stamping dance with a very timeless and exotic flavor.

The opening theme of the Sonata in E-flat Major, Wq 65/7, comes from the same family as that of Wq 65/1, but listen to how Bach expands the music's harmonic range. Only five years have passed but the additional degree of maturity is quite marked. As with the previous sonata, all three movements share the same mode—major this time—with the finale featuring an especially catchy, triple-time principal idea. The short G Minor Sonata, Wq 65/11, has a first movement that very strikingly anticipates the finale of Haydn's "Rider" Quartet, Op. 74 No. 3, also intriguingly in G minor. The resemblance is so telling that it's almost hard to imagine that Haydn didn't know this sonata. Perhaps it enjoyed some circulation in manuscript?

This group concludes with the very ear-catching Sonata in B Minor, Wq 65/13. The range of ideas in the first movement is impressive: there's a very strongly profiled but lyrical second subject in the major, rising and falling like a wave, and some particularly adventurous harmony, never mind the syncopated rhythms. After the first movement the Adagio is relatively serene, but the adventure continues in the Allegro molto finale. In short, this is a piece packed full of arresting ideas. At about eleven minutes, it's also one of Bach's more highly developed early works.

Group 2

Sonata in C Major, Wq 65/16 (1746)
Sonata in G Minor, Wq 65/17 (1746)
Sonata in B-flat Major, Wq 65/20 (1747)
Sonata in D Minor, Wq 65/24 (1749)
Sonata in C Minor, Wq 65/31 (1757)
Sonata in B-flat Major, Wq65/34 (1760)

I'm not sure what got into Bach in 1746, but the music of that year includes some of his most uninhibited and eccentric outpourings. This was also the year of the remarkable Keyboard Concerto in C Major, Wq 20, and the sonata in the same key, Wq 65/16, is just as daring. It's also one of his largest, lasting more than seventeen minutes. You're not going to believe what happens in the development section of the first movement, as the music grinds to a halt and pounds out a series of repeated chords in a remarkable act of romantic rhetorical excess. The slow movement violates every aspect of the "single affect" rule that it can. It starts normally enough, with a lyrical Adagio, but this is interrupted by extremely loud, vocal outbursts in unison octaves and in a quicker tempo. The music then proceeds in dialogue, flowing directly into the Allegretto finale—music whose unorthodoxies include more of those stern interruptions from the previous movement. This is Bach at his "in your face" best.

If the C Major Sonata is astonishing, then the G Minor, Wq 65/17, another very large work, seems simply incredible. Its first movement sounds like a free fantasia, with arresting musical gestures and rhythmic patterns rather than actual themes. The piece is through-composed, with no repeats, but also enough recapitulation to give a clear "sonata" feel. The Adagio follows without a break: music of great passion with a surprise ending that's pure poetry. I mentioned on a couple of other occasions that Bach sometimes seems to jump forward to the neoclassicism of more modern composers, and if someone suggested Prokofiev as the author of this finale, I would take the notion seriously. It's an absolutely nutty essay in harmonic ambiguity, but in the best possible and most entertaining way. There's nothing else really like it in eighteenth-century music.

Another big sonata, Wq 65/20 in B-flat Major, has a first movement with something of the improvisational qualities of the G Minor Sonata's opening alongside the harmonic kinks of that work's finale. It's almost jazzy in spots. The Adagio is very dreamy and ethereal, while the finale pretends to normalcy until some decidedly wrong note harmony throws the music off kilter. It's very funny, almost tipsy, writing.

Humor is the farthest thing from Bach's mind in Wq 65/24 in D Minor. This work has a most unusual form: Adagio, then Andantino, then Adagio again, with a quick interlude toward the end. The first Adagio has an ABA, minor-major-minor shape, with some grandly rhetorical gestures in the form of loud dissonant chords. The Andantino continues in much the same declamatory vein, and so does the finale, which sounds strikingly like an anticipation of the opening of Beethoven's "Pathétique" Piano Sonata. Only about seven minutes long, the music has a single-minded intensity unique in Bach's output.

Marked "Allegro assai ma pomposo" (very fast but pompous), the first movement of the Sonata in C Minor, Wq 65/31, has an eerie but also oddly humorous character. The Andantino is a dialogue between loud proclamations and more lyrical answers—it could have been a concerto movement, had an orchestra been on hand to take over one side of the conversation. It stays mainly in minor keys as well, and one source aptly designates it "Andantino pathetico." Bach describes the finale as a "joking allegro" (Allegro scherzando), and like the first movement it features a very curious mixture of seriousness and wit. We are operating at an extremely sophisticated level of expressive subtlety here.

Staying for a moment with the idea of pomposity, Bach marks the opening of the Sonata in B-flat Major, Wq 65/34, "Allegro pomposo." It is music full of ruffles and flourishes, more blatantly funny than the previous sonata, but the idea is similar. The word *pomposo* also can mean "showy" or "flashy," and perhaps that is the better translation. The Andante arioso slow movement, though, is simply vocal music of touching beauty from start to finish. As for the finale, by this time Bach has mastered the paradoxical art of writing music both relaxed but nevertheless interestingly vivid at one and the same time. This Allegretto offers a perfect case in point.

Group 3

Sonata in E-flat Major, Wq65/42 (1765)
Sonata in B-flat Major, Wq 65/44 (1766)
Sonata in E Major, Wq 65/46 (1766)
Sonata in C Major, Wq 65/47 (1775)
Sonata in G Major, Wq 65/48 (1783)
Sonata in G Major/A Minor, Wq 65/50 (1786)

All of the sonatas in this group are at least technically in major keys. As I mentioned previously, by this period Bach's mature harmonic style was so free that (as with Haydn) the home key mattered less than where the music wants to go and how it intends to get there. These late sonatas demonstrate this principle very clearly, starting with the hearty and wholesome first movement of the Sonata in E-flat Major, Wq 65/42. Note how the range of contrast in harmony and rhythm is as broad as ever, but it's all integrated into a particularly strong forward flow. Little need be said about the slow movement. When Bach describes a piece as "Adagio assai, sostenuto e affetuoso," you can always count on getting exactly the experience advertised. The finale is a delightful essay in what can be done with a descending major scale.

The Sonata in B-flat Major, Wq 65/44, has only two movements, but they are relatively large, playing for about twelve minutes combined, and the first movement features varied repeats. As you may have noticed, Bach often loves to start off a piece innocently, and then let the unusual incidents pile up, as happens in this Andantino. The finale is another example of Bach in "pointillist" mode, with strategically placed wrong-note chords that send the music careening off in unexpected and unexplained directions. This is notably dry humor, witty and very refreshing.

At nearly twenty minutes, the Sonata in E Major, Wq 65/46, may be Bach's single biggest. Marked "Allegro di molto," the opening sounds more like a lyrical slow movement, except for its tendency to take off like a shot, without warning. Almost ten minutes long, the piece is very extensively developed—a real musical journey, this. The central Larghetto retains the major key, only to use it as a springboard for moments of increasing poignancy. A very substantial final Allegro tries to conceal a certain lack of confidence with brave gestures and loud exclamations, but it finally retires graciously, piano.

The first movement of the Sonata in C Major, Wq 65/47, is very funny in a spastic sort of way. It's one of Bach's essays in deliberate eccentricity, with themes and motives that never seem to come out the same way twice. The very brief, transitional, harmonically ambiguous Adagio assai flows directly into a finale that returns to the same hijinks as we heard in the first movement. If you are listening carefully, you might notice that this Andante is, in fact, a variation of the sonata's opening. The result is music at once almost garishly disjoined and strongly unified—an audible paradox if ever there was one.

Another fine example of seemingly gentle music that at the same time sustains a remarkable level of suspense, Wq 65/48's opening Andantino mixes lyrical charm with something considerably stronger. The short Adagio e sostenuto slow movement leads to very harmonically disturbed (and disturbing) finale. We really don't know how, or even if, the music will end, but it does so with a wink and a sly grin. This sonata, by the way, is the one that Bach designated to be played by the bowed harpsichord, the so-called *Bogen-Clavier*, but there's no evidence from the music alone that suggests the piece is not suitable to whatever keyboard instrument happens to be available.

Bach describes the first movement of the last sonata in this group, Wq 65/50 in G Major, as a rondo, and that is exactly what it is—a very short one less than three minutes in length. The hymnlike Andante retains the major mode and incorporates some surprisingly sharp dissonances without breaking its stride. Bach cataloguer E. Eugene Helm describes this sonata as in G major/A minor because the finale very surprisingly starts in the minor and goes back and forth between modes seemingly with every phrase. The minor wins in the end. And so a little sonata barely seven minutes long, which started out sounding so harmless, decides to get serious at the very last minute.

"Farewell to My Silbermann Clavichord," in a Rondo (Rondo in E minor), Wq 66 (1781)

Bach couldn't have been that attached to his beloved Silbermann clavichord, or he would not have sold it. Certainly he didn't need the money at this point in his career. Whether or not we take the musical result seriously, or treat is as a melodramatically tragic bit of dark humor, the result is a quite spectacularly gloomy meditation on loneliness and loss. The notation is full of vibrato indications, a sure sign of deep emotion, and the piece is clearly geared toward Bach's favored instrument. I tend to hear this piece as tongue in cheek. It is just *so* exaggeratedly glum, which doesn't alter that fact that he wrote it with perfect seriousness. After all, great humor is always serious, and the music works either way.

Free Fantasia for Keyboard in F-sharp Minor "Carl Philipp Emanuel Bach's Emotions," Wq 67

This piece has already been discussed in detail as one of the works included in the accompanying track listing.

Sonata in D Minor, Wq 69 (1747—for harpsichord with two manuals)

The outstanding feature of this sonata is the long finale, a theme and variations (nine of them), for each of which Bach specifies the remarkable range of tone colors available on the instrument for which it was written. Modern performances sound best on the piano, where the variety of touch and dynamics can at least approximate the timbral resources that the composer must have had in mind, but the variations themselves have plenty of character no matter what the instrument actually chosen. The preceding two movements—a dynamic opening Allegro and a lyrical Andante in the major, with occasional passionate outbursts—are much shorter. This finale is, in fact, the longest in any Bach sonata, with a duration exceeding that of the two previous movements combined.

Six Sonatas and One Prelude for Organ, Wq 70 (1755)

No. 1 in A Major (1758)
No. 2 in B-flat Major (1758)
No. 3 in F Major
No. 4 in A Minor
No. 5 in D Major
No. 6 in G Minor
No. 7 Prelude in D Major

The Princess Anna Amalia was very conservative, and had an organ installed in her living room so as to avail herself of the "learned style" of such composers as Bach's father. C. P. E. wrote his organ sonatas for her, but there is little evidence that she played them or acknowledged the dedication. They would almost certainly have been too radical for her taste, although she apparently enjoyed the Sonatas with Varied Reprises. Wotquenne identified six organ sonatas and one prelude, but later scholarship has determined that Wq 70/1 in A Major was actually written for a standard keyboard instrument. It reappears as Wq 65/32.

The confusion arose in part because Bach's organ writing here does not make use of the pedals, and so is difficult to distinguish from his normal keyboard style. In fact, he wrote very little of importance for the organ; these pieces and the two concertos about do it, aside from a few smaller items (such as the Six Fugues, Wq 119/2–7). These sonatas have been recorded: most notably by the baroque organ music specialist

Herbert Tachezi, and with the exception of the pithy Sonata in B-flat Major, all six are substantial works lasting around twelve minutes each.

There are some very fine pieces here, especially the Sonatas in A Minor and D Major, with their driving outer movements and expressive Adagios. The problem with C. P. E. Bach on the organ is that the music is very dependent on the technical limitations of the instrument on which it is played. In particular, many organs really "speak" too slowly, and permit too little variety of articulation to capture Bach's speed of pacing, abruptness of rhythm, and range of phrasing. The result can turn heavy and sluggish. In the Sonata in F Major, for example, rather than sounding witty and full of contrast, the piece comes across as merely disjointed, or at least that has been my (admittedly limited) impression.

Organ music is, in any case, very much an acquired taste for most modern listeners, and as with all of Bach's keyboard music these pieces are perfectly playable, and probably sound better on the contemporaneous alternatives, never mind the modern piano. Any possible sacrifice of the organ's sustaining power in a few passages would be more than compensated for in terms of most other musical parameters. Ultimately, only time will tell if these pieces will acquire a reputation on a par with Bach's other major sonata collections. Certainly the music shows him writing at the top of his form, and it would be a shame if the designation "organ sonata" prevents these pieces from gaining the attention that they surely deserve.

Arioso with 5 Variations in A Major, Wq 79 (1781)

This piece also exists in a version for keyboard with violin. It's a fine work, largely because the theme is so long and intricate that the variations are more like varied reprises. All kinds of typically Bach-like things happen as the music explores the theme, especially in terms of unexpected harmonies and interesting changes in musical direction. One version or the other of Wq 79 is certainly worth hearing, and happily both have enjoyed multiple recordings. The only issue with this piece, as with Bach's variation forms more generally, is that they don't build to a climax leading to a particularly satisfying ending. Each variation remains a self-contained unit, and when they are done the music simply stops, often abruptly.

Minuet in C Major, Wq 111 (1731)

This is Bach's first published work, just ninety seconds long. As such, it surely deserves its own Wq number. It would be lovely to say that it contains anticipations of everything that came later, but who are we kidding? It's lively, charming, rhythmically interesting, not really dancelike at all, and that's the entire story.

Keyboard Pieces of Various Types, Wq 112

There are nineteen pieces in this collection, and for some reason twelve of them also wound up in Wq 116 and 117 (six in each). The most important work here is the Concerto in C Major, Wq 112/1, of 1765. This is a full-fledged concerto that Bach decided not to orchestrate, but to leave as a solo keyboard piece. The trick in listening is to figure out what parts belong to the orchestra and which get played "solo." If you sampled some of the works described in the chapter on the concertos, you should have a good feel for how ritornello form works and how this composer parcels out his musical ideas. The music itself is fully mature Bach, with a first movement in which the solo and orchestra have clearly differentiated ideas—a particularly sensible strategy when there's no additional ensemble to provide timbral contrast. A very dramatic, minor-key Largo precedes the humorous finale, which features some particularly well-timed jokes.

The other major work in this collection is the Sonata in D Minor, Wq 112/7. All three movements share the piece's basic minor-key coloration. The opening Allegretto is memorably pathetic and lyrical, while the central Poco adagio e mesto really is as sad as Bach suggests. The finale has the same brooding melancholy as the first movement, only with a harder edge. Other pieces only found in Wq 112 include a transcription for keyboard of the Symphony in G Major, Wq 180, three song arrangements, and the Fugue in G Minor, Wq 112/19.

Short and Easy Keyboard Pieces with Varied Reprises, Volumes 1 and 2, Wq 113 and 114 (1765/67)

Each of these sets consists of eleven tiny pieces, including minuets, polonaises, allegros, andantes, and two fantasias, both in D minor, and both also are included in Wq 117. Although most of the items only last about a minute each, some a bit more, some a bit less, the music is more interesting than you might think if only because it really does give an excellent sense of how Bach expected repetitions to be varied. True, our interest will be more technical than emotional, directed to process rather than expression, but as teaching pieces these are very well designed and full of simple charm.

Volume of Minuets, Polonaises, and Different Pieces for Keyboard, Wq 116

Composed mostly in the 1750s and '60s, this collection, twenty-eight items in all, contains basically the same mixed assortment of pieces as Wq 113 and 114. They require no additional discussion; you will know how much of this kind of thing you need.

Volume of Solfeggios, Fantasias, and Character Pieces for Keyboard, Wq 117

There are forty pieces in this collection, including the Solfeggio in C Minor and "L'Aly Rupalich," both featured in the listening samples accompanying this book. Bach's character pieces date from the mid-1750s, and take as their models the French keyboard works of Rameau and Couperin, among others. Bach composed twenty-five in all (twenty-six if we include "L'Ernestine," Wq 199/16) and unlike the French models, Bach's are mostly shorter, simpler, and only one—"Les Langueurs tendres"—is not an obvious character sketch. The truth is that Bach disliked musical illustration, believing that the purpose of music was to evoke the passions, not to imitate or describe extra-musical imagery. His character pieces are, nevertheless, very entertaining, and in addition to the complete set selections also have been recorded as individual programs.

One way to explore them is to listen to the versions that that Bach arranged and inserted into the orchestral sonatinas. You can find these discussed in Chapter 4. If you enjoyed "L'Aly Rupalich," there is even another murky ("La Böhmer") in this set; and fans of the Solfeggietto in C Minor will be pleased to know that it also has two companions, both just a touch shorter. The six fantasias included here (if we count the two on loan from Wq 112) are babies compared to those in the *Kenner und Liebhaber* volumes, but there's much to be said for using these pieces as Bach intended—to help us grow accustomed to bigger and more sophisticated works built along similar lines.

Volume of Various Keyboard Pieces with Variations, Wq 118

Bach wrote variation sets throughout his career, but the form received less attention from him than you might expect. The reason, undoubtedly, stems from the fact that the variation *concept* was already so integral to his compositional aesthetic that he saw little use for full-scale works that bear the actual name. Nevertheless, some of his variation sets are very extensive and reward attentive listening. Here are the works included in Wq 118:

- Variations on "Ich schlief, da träumte mir" [17 Variations], Wq 118/1
- Second set of Variations on "Ich schlief, da träumte mir" [7 Variations], Wq 118/1
- Ariette in A Major [17 Variations], Wq 118/2
- Second set of Variations on the Ariette in A Major [5 Variations], Wq 118/2
- Minuet in C Major [5 Variations], Wq 118/3
- Arioso in F Major [7 Variations], Wq 118/4
- Allegretto in C Major [6 Variations], Wq 118/5
- Variations on "Colin à peine à seize ans" [12 Variations], Wq 118/6
- Minuet in G Major by Pietro Locatelli [18 Variations], Wq 118/7

- Variations on a Canzonetta in F Major by the Duchess of Gotha [6 Variations], Wq 118/8
- Variations on "Les Folies d'Espagne" [12 Variations], Wq 118/9
- Arioso in C Major [9 Variations], Wq 118/10

Perhaps the most purely Bachian work here is Wq 118/9, because "Les Folies d'Espagne," better known in Italian simply as "La Folia," is such a well-known tune and Bach's handling of it is correspondingly individual. Just about every major composer in the baroque period wrote variations on it; most famously Corelli, and his setting in turn became the subject of one of Rachmaninov's greatest piano pieces, the "Corelli" Variations. Because, as mentioned previously, Bach's variations tend to remain independent and he makes little effort to bind them together into larger units or create a sense of climax at the end (other than the inherent unity of the concept, of course), his works in this medium are particularly easy to follow. If you enjoyed the Arioso with Variations in A Major, Wq 79, or the finale of the Sonata in D Minor, Wq 69, then any of these pieces will give much satisfaction.

With Wq 118, we come to the end of this survey of all of the major keyboard works. There are a few other odds and ends that you can find in Table 3 that accompanies this discussion, and follow them up at your leisure. I hope you have gotten a sense of what an incredible legacy this really is. The point is not that you should feel any necessity to spend countless hours listening to all of it—unless, of course, you really want to—but rather that you can dip in just about anywhere and find something absolutely terrific to occupy however much time you have to spare. You don't even have to plan ahead. Just "drop the needle" (as we used to say in the old LP days), hit Shuffle, or do whatever is easiest to put yourself in contact with the music. It's that good.

Chamber Music

When I completed my academic studies in 1738 and went to Berlin, I received a very favorable opportunity to escort a young nobleman on his travels abroad. The journey I was planning was cancelled when I was unexpectedly and graciously summoned to Ruppin by the then Crown Prince (now King) of Prussia. Certain circumstances, however, led to my not formally entering the Prussian service until 1740, when His Majesty's reign began, and I alone was favored to accompany on the harpsichord the first flute solo His Majesty played as king in Charlottenburg Palace.

—C. P. E. Bach, *Autobiography*[20]

There is a wonderful but possibly apocryphal story concerning Bach's relationship with Frederick the Great that speaks directly to his chamber music output. At a recital in which Frederick played the flute to Bach's accompaniment, a spectator supposedly complimented the king, saying, "What rhythm!" to which the composer countered, "What rhythms!" Whereas Quantz, the more diplomatic courtier, got along famously with his employer, Bach evidently did not. He was unimpressed by Frederick's musicianship, and Frederick disliked Bach's compositions. Nevertheless, Bach remained with the king for thirty years, so there must have been at least some degree of mutual respect and toleration. Frederick knew genuine talent when he saw it, and Bach was certainly not foolish enough to push his boss too far.

Table 4: Chamber Music

Wq or H#	Title/Scoring	Notes/Translations
	Solo Sonatas (17)	
Wq 132	Solo Flute	
Wq 123–134	Flute and Basso Continuo	
Wq 135	Oboe and Basso Continuo	
Wq 136–137	Viola da gamba and Basso Continuo	
Wq 139	Harp and Basso Continuo	usually performed as a solo
	Trio Sonatas (23)	
Wq 143–153	Flute, Violin, and Bass	
Wq 154–160	2 Violins and Bass	
Wq 161/1	2 Violins and Bass	"Conversation between a happy person (Sanguineus) and a sad person (Melancholicus)"
Wq 161/2	Flute, Violin, and Bass	
Wq 162	2 Flutes and Bass	
Wq 163	Bass Recorder, Viola, and Bass	
H 585	2 Violins and Bass	
	Keyboard Trios (16)	
Wq 71–78	Keyboard and Violin	
Wq 79	Keyboard and Violin	Arioso with Variations in A Major
Wq 80	Keyboard and Violin	Fantasia in F-sharp Minor "C. P. E. Bach's Emotions" (also for solo keyboard, Wq 67)
Wq 83–87	Keyboard and Flute	
Wq 88	Keyboard and Viola da gamba	

continued

Wq or H#	Title/Scoring	Notes/Translations
	Accompanied Sonatas (13)	
Wq 89	Six sonatas pour le clavecin ou piano forte accompagnées d'un violon & violoncelle	Six sonatas for harpsicord or piano accompanied by violin and cello
Wq 90	Claviersonaten mit einer Violine und einem Violoncell zur Begleitung, Erste Sammlung (3)	Keyboard Sonatas with a Violin and Cello Accompaniment, First Volume
Wq 91	Claviersonaten mit einer Violine und einem Violoncell zur Begleitung, Zweyte Sammlung (4)	Keyboard Sonatas with a Violin and Cello Accompaniment, Second Volume (3 Sonatas and 1 Arioso)
	Quartets (3)	
Wq 93–95	Fortepiano, Flute, and Viola	
	Potentially Interesting Other Stuff (if you can find it)	
Wq 81	Kleine Stücke mit Zwei und Drei Stimmen (12)	Little Pieces in Two and Three Parts (2 Flutes or 2 Flutes and Continuo)
Wq 82	Kleine Stücke mit Zwei und Drei Stimmen (12)	Little Pieces in Two and Three Parts (2 Flutes or 2 Flutes and Continuo)
Wq 92	Sonatas for Keyboard, Clarinet, and Bassoon (6)	
Wq 140	Duet for Flute and Violin	
Wq 142	Duet for Two Clarinets	
Wq 184	Sonatas for Two Horns, Two Flutes, Two Clarinets, and Bassoon (6)	
Wq 185	Marches for Two Horns, Two Oboes, Two Clarinets, and Bassoon (6)	
Wq 187	Marches for Two Horns, Two Oboes, and Bassoon (2)	

continued

Wq or H#	Title/Scoring	Notes/Translations
Wq 188	March for Three Trumpets and Timpani	
Wq 189/1–2	Minuets for Two Flutes, Two Clarinets, Two Violins, and Bass (2)	
Wq 189/3–6	Minuets for Two Flutes, Two Violins, and Bass	
Wq 190	Polonaises for Two Horns, Two Clarinets, Two Violins, and Bass (6)	Nos. 2, 3, 5, 6 for Two Violins and Bass; No. 1 add Clarinets; No. 4 full ensemble
Wq 191/192	Minuets for Three Trumpets, Timpani, Two Horns, Two Oboes, Two Flutes, Two Violins, Viola, and Bass (2)	
Wq 193	Pieces for Mechanical Instruments (29)	

Their non-relationship probably explains why, although Bach wrote a great deal of chamber music for the flute, there is no evidence that Frederick played any of it, and no particularly noteworthy surge of new flute pieces such as we see coming from Quantz or, indeed, Frederick himself. The flute was a fashionable instrument throughout the eighteenth century; the fact that the king played it, and played it well (Bach's comments notwithstanding), only would have made it more so, especially in Berlin. Bach's chamber music, then, consists of works composed relatively steadily throughout his career and includes pieces for all of the usual combinations of the day—and several unusual ones as well.

Bach began writing chamber music at the very start of his career. In the early 1770s he purposefully destroyed all of the music that he regarded as immature, and as we have already seen much of the rest of his output from the 1730s was revised, or "renovated," during his Berlin years. This is particularly true of his chamber works. There was, evidently, a single piece written in partnership with his father that Bach took care to preserve, but it was never published and it disappeared after his death.

In considering the chamber works, there are some special considerations that we need to take into account. The principal medium for small ensemble pieces in Bach's day was the trio sonata for two melody instruments, usually of the same range, plus continuo. This means two violins, two flutes, or flute and violin. The continuo group often consisted of keyboard plus a cello or other "low" instrument to reinforce the bass line. A "trio" thus accommodated four players, or even more depending on who was accompanying. What made it a trio was the fact that there were three principal musical lines, or voices: the two melody instruments plus the bass. Anything else was filler.

However, in the hands of such composers as Bach, who began to emancipate the role of the keyboard from that of mere accompaniment, the trio sonata could also contract down to as few as two players: a single melody instrument, the right hand of the keyboard as the second melody instrument, and the left hand keeping the bass. Today, we would call these just sonatas for whichever instrument was not the keyboard: flute sonata, violin sonata, and so on. The scoring was thus flexible, and quite a few of Bach's chamber works exploit this fact. He arranged solo sonatas as trios, and trios as solos, all the while preserving the basic three-part texture.

The form of these pieces is exactly what we find in Bach's keyboard sonatas, and so needs no additional discussion here. Originally, earlier in the eighteenth century, trio sonatas often had four movements organized slow-fast-slow-fast, but Bach and many of his colleagues preferred the three movement, fast-slow-fast format, sometimes called concerto style for obvious reasons. Solo sonatas, on the other hand, took the shape that we find in many of his sonatinas for keyboard and orchestra: slow-fast-fast (dance), and this format would be retained no matter what the actual disposition of instruments in later arrangements.

Because of the often-incestuous relationship between Bach's chamber works, it makes little sense to discuss in detail everything in the complete chamber music list in Table 4 at the head of this chapter. The situation with recordings also differs from those of Bach's other instrumental pieces. Despite today's mania for complete editions, the irregular numbers that characterize the individual groups of works mean that the discography consists primarily of single discs containing any number of miscellaneous pieces culled from the various media in which C. P. E. worked. Even where it is possible to respect the integrity of a specific set, as in the Three Quartets, Wq 93–95, the music is too short to fill a disc, and so requires additional material to round out the program. This can make any attempt at systematic collecting frustrating, as well as prone to duplication.

Therefore, in considering the best way to approach the chamber works I have opted to consider in detail a dozen of the most interesting and representative examples, which I also know can be sourced with relative ease. In seeking them out, you will inevitably also acquire other pieces, and have the opportunity to get to know them as well.

The biggest gap in the current discography concerns the Accompanied Sonatas, Wq 89–91. These are essentially keyboard sonatas reinforced by violin and cello, similar conceptually to many of Haydn's piano trios. They can thus be played as keyboard solos simply by leaving out the string parts. Bach wrote thirteen of them between 1775 and 1777. They sold very well, and they are certainly worth hearing. Only a few have been recorded, and those may be very hard to find. Now that the music has been published in the Complete Works, new recordings will doubtless appear eventually. You may want to keep an eye out for them.

Two Unusual Solos

Sonata for Solo Flute in A Minor, Wq 132 (1747)
Sonata for Harp in G Major, Wq 139 (1762)

The obvious model for Bach's Sonata for Solo Flute is his father's Partita for Solo Flute, BWV 1013, in the same key of A minor. Solo flute music is rare, and great solo flute music is even rarer. This is great solo flute music, and a surprisingly large work, too—about twelve minutes in three movements, an adagio followed by two allegros. J. S. Bach taught us that the size of a piece need not have anything to do with the mere number of players involved. His largest continuous movement must be the grandiose Chaconne from the D Minor Partita for Solo Violin. That alone plays for some fifteen to twenty minutes, so we shouldn't be surprised when his son writes a full-scale sonata for the solo flute.

The date of composition suggests that Bach wrote the piece for King Frederick, but the story goes that when blind flutist Friedrich Ludwig Dülon (1769–1826) visited Bach in 1783 and played the work for him, the composer said, "The person I wrote it for couldn't play it, and the one I didn't write it for can." This comment has set off a flurry of scholarly speculation, with some pointing out that Frederick may not have been the intended recipient at all, and others noting the king's dislike of Bach's music generally. It's also worth speculating that "couldn't" may not refer to technical ability, but might also mean "couldn't be bothered" to do it. We don't know.

In any event, one of the most noteworthy elements in any piece for a solo melody instrument, whether a violin, cello, or the flute, is how Bach manages to suggest fuller harmony than we actually hear by touching in a bass line with wide skips in register and writing themes that imply their own harmonization. This is easier in quick movements than in slow because the abundance of rapid figuration provides plenty of opportunities to toss in extra notes "in passing." With a wind instrument, particularly in slow music, the need to sustain the breath and create a singing line can be very taxing, and for that reason the opening Adagio is the shortest movement of the three. That Bach surmounts the technical limitations of his chosen medium and still creates an affecting (and not dull) musical experience, just as his father did before him, offers further proof of his individual genius.

If solo flute music is rare, then solo harp music in this period is rarer still. There's some controversy as to whether Bach's Harp Sonata requires a continuo accompaniment, but today you are much more likely to hear it played purely as a solo. Frankly it is somewhat difficult to imagine the point of combining a harp with a harpsichord, but then we don't have the sound of early harps in mind, so perhaps it would work. Either way, what Bach has composed is essentially a keyboard sonata, but with the structure of a chamber music solo: Adagio un poco—Allegro—Allegro. Here, without the problems of breath control, the opening slow movement is the largest, but this is still a full-size piece in all other respects. If you enjoy harp music, this is the only eighteenth-century piece written for the instrument that anyone cares about.

Two Alternate Versions for Violin and Keyboard

Arioso in A Major, Wq 79 (1781)
Fantasie in F-sharp Minor, Wq 80 "C. P. E. Bach's Emotions" (1787)

The addition of the violin to Bach's keyboard originals turns these two works, technically, into "trios," even though they make no effort to maintain anything like a strict, three-part texture. The violin plays a subordinate role in both; Bach seems to have added it primarily to enhance the music's singing qualities by sustaining long notes and accentuating key melodic phrases. Despite having a main key of A major, the Arioso begins rather sadly, but becomes more cheerful as the music progresses through the five ensuing variations.

The violin version of Wq 79 is basically the same as that for keyboard solo, but this is not true of the Fantasie, Wq 80. In the first place, the addition of the violin has required Bach to add bar lines to keep the two players together, but more important, instead of ending in darkness the violin version concludes with an entirely new movement in quick tempo, and in a major key. The music isn't exactly cheerful, but its 6/8 meter is refreshingly lilting and the general message seems to be one of consolation in adversity. Bach characteristically links the two movements together, and he might just as well have called the result a sonata, particularly as this new music appears to have originated in the finale of the Sonata in G Major, Wq 58/2.

There's an interesting topic for speculation in connection with this version of the Fantasia: it's the place where we find "C. P. E. Bach's Emotions" added as an explanatory title. It could be that Bach did not want this personal expression of his feelings to conclude so sadly, and so he reserved the moniker for this healthier and more expressively balanced revision. It's always worth remembering that even the most emotionally turbulent composers generally were not crazed depressives, and that Bach's life, while certainly not devoid of sadness, was for the most part a happy and fulfilling one right until the end.

Three Keyboard Trios (with Violin)

Sonata in B Minor, Wq 76 (1763)
Sonata in B-flat Major, Wq 77 (1763)
Sonata in C Minor, Wq 78 (1763)

There is actually a fourth (or first) sonata that belongs to this group: Wq 75 in F Major, and the only reason I have left it out of this discussion is that there is a superb recording of the above three works, conveniently coupled with the Arioso in A Major, featuring German violinist Albrecht Breuninger accompanied by fortepianist Piet Kuijken on the Hänssler Classic label. Given the situation with C. P. E.'s chamber works on disc, I felt it made sense to opt for maximum convenience, but please don't take my omission of Wq 75 as a suggestion of its inferiority on my part.

These pieces are true gems, and although they technically belong under the rubric of "trio," they are for all intents and purposes violin sonatas in the modern sense: true duos between two equal partners. This is all the more remarkable in considering Wq 76, which was composed in 1731 as a trio sonata for flute and violin, revised for that combination in 1747 (as Wq 143), and only later refashioned as it appears here.

The first movement makes it very clear what Bach's contemporaries meant by the three-movement "concerto style." The piece opens with what is effectively a ritornello for the keyboard, after which the violin enters with independent material. Trio textures return in the Poco andante, a dialogue between the violin and the accompanist's right hand. For the finale, Bach offers a very Italianate Allegretto siciliano, one of those pieces which, although it remains mostly in a minor key, sounds more exotic and dancelike than it does sad or pathetic. At nearly twenty minutes, this sonata isn't merely in "concerto style;" it's concerto length, too.

Wq 77 is the most brilliant and vivacious of the group. Its outer movements are marked "Allegro di molto" and "Presto," respectively, and the piece starts with virtuoso fiddling right off the bat. The two players suffer several moments of humorous confusion as the movement proceeds, but it all comes out well in the end. A very sad central largo leads to the wacky concluding Presto, which features some very tricky rhythms in its main theme. Once again Bach plays with our expectations in sudden moments of hesitation that keep us guessing right up to the end.

The Sonata in C Minor, Wq 78, is a very major work, more than twenty minutes long. Its big opening Allegro moderato features a deeply affecting main theme that actually seems to weep, especially when given to the violin. The slow movement, Adagio ma non troppo, is just heavenly: rippling arpeggios from the keyboard introduce a seraphic, romantic strain on the muted violin. This music is timeless; it could have been composed a century later, and it mirrors the mood and atmosphere we hear in pieces like the Nocturne of Borodin's String Quartet No. 2.

The concluding Presto is a perpetual motion piece in tarantella rhythm—another case of the minor key used for color and character as well as pathos. There's one big moment of surprise toward the end, when the music comes to sudden and shocking halt before the breakaway conclusion. This is a remarkable sonata by any standard, surely one of Bach's greatest. Many moments have a thoroughly modern sound, and musically it can more than hold its own with anything on one of today's chamber music programs. It deserves to be much better known.

One note of caution: beware of performances on period instruments that adopt the current orthodoxy with regard to string technique. The slow movement, especially, demands the kind of healthy, singing tone with plenty of vibrato on sustained notes that so many contemporary artists avoid on principle, in plain defiance of what period treatises and aesthetics demand. It's a fine test of whether the violin player is a musician or a robot.

Three Quartets (for harpsichord, flute, and viola)

Quartet in A Minor, Wq 93 (1788)
Quartet in D Major, Wq 94 (1788)
Quartet in G Major, Wq 95 (1788)

We owe the existence of these pieces, Bach's last works, once again to wealthy patron and keyboardist Sarah Levy, who commissioned them for her own use. Bach called them quartets, and so they are, since both hands of the keyboard player get counted. In some performances, a cello may double the bass line. It has no independent part, but the music sounds better with it. Scored for the remarkable combination of flute and viola (Levy's husband played the flute), these pieces have a color and character like no other music of the period. They are quite clearly "late" works. Bach's use of the instruments has a clarity of texture and an almost pointillist subtlety of shading, with musical lines effortlessly tossed back and forth between the players.

All three quartets share the same basic structure: an opening movement in moderate tempo (Andantino, and two Allegrettos), a very slow middle (Large e sostenuto and two Adagios), and a very quick finale (Allegro assai, Allegro di molto, and Presto). Wq 93 opens with one of Bach's minor-key march themes, very similar to the one at the start of the Symphony for Strings in B Minor, Wq 182/5. The two remaining quartets feature deeply pathetic slow movements, and the finales of each really are memorable. That of Wq 93 is very quirky and full of sardonic humor, while the D Major Quartet's last movement has a Haydn-esque sense of fun. In the conclusion of Wq 95 all three (or four) players join in a truly virtuosic romp. As with his last keyboard concerto, also for Sarah Levy, Bach clearly decided to go out with a laugh.

Two Trio Sonatas

Trio Sonata for Bass Recorder, Viola, and Continuo in F Major, Wq 163 (1755)
Trio Sonata for Two Violins and Continuo in C Minor, Wq 161/1 "Conversation between a happy person (Sanguineus) and a sad person (Melancholicus)" (1749)

We conclude this selection of chamber works with two of Bach's most distinctive trio sonatas. Wq 163 probably has one of the most convoluted histories of anything that he wrote. It began life as a Trio Sonata in B-flat Major, Wq 159, for two violins and keyboard. It then got arranged, possibly spuriously, as a sonata for single violin and continuo (H. 543), then for bass recorder, viola, and continuo, with the possibility of a bassoon replacing the viola as an alternative. It is, in any event, a curious piece, first in that it adopts solo sonata structure: Un poco andante—Allegretto—Allegro. The gradual acceleration in tempo actually complements the dark scoring of the revised version and prevents the music from sounding drab. The hollow tone of the bass recorder, combined with the husky viola, makes for a most unique array of timbres. While the overall tone of the piece is cheerful and mellow, Bach's revision for "low" instruments adds an oddly disquieting undertone.

The Trio Sonata for Two Violins and Continuo in C Minor, Wq 161/1, depicting a conversation between two gentlemen, one cheerful, the other sad, became one of Bach's most famous pieces. It was, clearly, an experiment, and in later life he seems to have regretted it. His preface to the sonata, in which he explains his purpose, sounds somewhat defensive and very concerned that his intentions may be misunderstood. It makes delightful reading, and deserves to be quoted in full:

> In the first trio the attempt has been made to express with instruments, as much as possible, what would otherwise more comfortably be achieved with the singing voice and words. It should represent, as it were, a dialogue between a Sanguineus and a Melancholicus, who argue with each other for the entire

> first movement and until nearly the end of the second movement, each trying to win over the other to his side, until they resolve their differences at the end of the second movement, when Melancholicus finally gives in and takes over the other's main theme.
>
> In the last movement they are and remain fully united, whereby nonetheless one can observe that Melancholicus begins with a theme that is rather jaunty, somewhat coquettish, but also somewhat languid and above all generally pathetic. Toward its end it shows a little spell of sadness which, however, is immediately banished—after a brief effective rest—by a few lively triplets. Sanguineus, who approves of the other's relenting, steadfastly follows in this last movement out of courtesy, even during the somewhat subdued passages; and both affirm their friendship by imitating each other, even to the point that one cannot tell them apart.
>
> In order to strike the right tempo in the first movement of this trio, one should note that in the Presto one measure must be played just as a triplet of three eighths would be played in the Allegretto; and that consequently a whole measure in the Presto takes no more time than a quarter does in the Allegretto.
>
> One will do well to play this first trio without the addition of any arbitrary ornamentation, but rather just as it is written. And if one wishes to play two of the parts on the keyboard it would make a good effect if the uppermost part (Sanguineus) along with the bass were taken, partly to retain the various expressions of Melancholicus, with and without mute, and partly because of the many long-held notes, which on the harpsichord or clavichord cannot be heard as they should be. This minor inconvenience does not apply to the second trio [Wq 161/2], as one can take the two lowest parts on the keyboard.
>
> In anticipation, no mockery will be tolerated for finding it necessary here to assist those who do not yet possess sufficient insight into the musical expression by adding some comments on the main places in the first two movements of this trio.[21]

There then follows a remarkable chart containing commentary on the music cued to letters in the score. This runs from letter A to RR, or almost twice through the alphabet. A sample:

(f) Here Sanguineus breaks off questioningly, whether Melancholicus wishes to continue with the missing material?

(g) Instead, Melancholicus slips in a snippet of his main theme.

(h) Sanguineus is unsure whether Melancholicus has done this out of malice, ignorance, or forgetfulness; therefore he shows him again how he should have responded, although with acrimony because he again prevents him from speaking his mind.

(i) Here Melancholicus begins to give in, and to answer correctly as he should have done earlier.[22]

And so it goes. Whether music can express any of this in such detail is, of course, a moot point. It seems to have taken Bach as much time and trouble to write the preface and explanatory notes as it did the entire piece, and it's no surprise that he never repeated the effort. Meanwhile, we have an absolutely delightful trio sonata, with a very schizophrenic first movement in two tempos featuring a Melancholicus who is sometimes muted, sometimes not, a brief slow movement that effects exactly the reconciliation that Bach describes, and a minor-key finale that the composer still characterizes as being on the sanguine side. It really is, although perhaps the minor mode also symbolizes the union of the two personalities: Sanguineus's energy and abandon with a touch of Melancholicus's sour attitude.

Bach's chamber works, perhaps more than any other area of his creative output, may strike us today as old-fashioned. This is because he stuck resolutely to the ensemble types that he inherited from the baroque period, even as Haydn and his colleagues were busy exploring a new paradigm in which small groups of instruments could play together with no harmonic support from a keyboard player, each participating in the musical discourse on an equal footing. This new conception of chamber music culminated in the classical string quartet. However, Bach's failure to follow this path should not blind us to the fact that his chamber pieces are still wholly characteristic and often magnificent, even if they do represent in certain cases an instance of the composer pouring new musical wine into old bottles.

9 Parting Thoughts

From now on I will publish nothing more myself. All my debts are now settled correctly. I am very satisfied. The writing of letters and keeping of accounts are inconvenient to me in my old age. It is somewhat different with you. I intend to write an introduction to composition according to the current times, *with the* necessary *rules and with* omission of all pedantry, *and with that, if God lets me live, I will close.*

—C. P. E. Bach letter to his publisher, Johann Breitkopf, 8 March 1788[23]

Alas, God did not let C. P. E. Bach live to complete this last project, though we may say with good reason that the music tells us as much as another treatise ever could. Having traced a path through the composer's voluminous output in a way that hopefully points you in a productive direction, I would like to close by sharing some personal reflections.

I have been writing about music for a long time now, since the mid-1980s, and I have been an enthusiastic classical music listener for much longer than that. For most of this time, C. P. E. Bach was a closed book to me. For starters, I have never been a huge fan of J. S. Bach. There are pieces that I truly enjoy: the Goldberg Variations, *The Well-Tempered Clavier*, the Magnificat and B-Minor Mass, a few cantatas and concertos; but on the whole, he is a composer whose work I respect more than love. I don't deny his greatness; no one who pretends to care about music or understand it could do that, but in truth I often find him intimidating, relentless, and the worshipful attitude of so much of the musical establishment frankly turns me off. I realize that admitting this is like declaring yourself to be an atheist at the Southern Baptist Convention, but there it is.

I expected much the same from C. P. E. After all, he was nothing if not a devoted son, and heir to the same tradition. What little I heard of him on recordings always was presented in the shadow of his father. His D Minor Concerto, Wq 23, was the successor to J. S. Bach's BWV 1052, only less so. How could the later setting of the Magnificat compare to the earlier one? The fact that C. P. E. wrote no operas, whether any good or not, simply made him look like an anachronistic grump, a historical curiosity catering to an equally grim, humorless North German Lutheran middle class. His music sounded neither fully baroque, nor Viennese, and I only heard it for what is wasn't, rather than for what it was.

This situation was only exacerbated in the 1970s, '80s and '90s by the great baroque revival that swamped the recording industry in connection with the rise of the Historically Informed Performance movement. Suddenly, all of these composers who had only been names in textbooks started showing up: Corelli, Geminiani, Telemann, Locatelli, Tartini, Pachelbel, Vivaldi, and countless others. RCA released a disc called *Pachelbel's Greatest Hit*, which consisted of nothing but arrangements of the already ubiquitous Canon in D, including a vocal version by Cleo Laine (the words went something like, "Who, where, why, when will we touch again?") and a movement from a George Rochberg string quartet. Vivaldi's *The Four Seasons* got played on public radio every fifteen minutes, with maybe a Bach Brandenburg Concerto offered for relief every so often.

Now, it's true that Veracini does not sound exactly like Albinoni, but it's equally the case that much of this music comes across as very similar, and as a record critic I began to dread yet another recording of sonatas or concertos for violin or flute or oboe, plus continuo, of course, scratched or tweeted out by Ye Royale Majestey's Consortt of Merriye Musicians of St. Throckmorton-on-Tisdale, or whatever flavor-of-the-week pickup ensemble (they all used the same players—only the name changed) was being pushed by the major labels. Then in 1991 we had

"The Mozart Year," and all hell broke loose. There was a complete edition. There were multiple issues of music he wrote when he was six. There were new reconstructions of the unfinished Requiem. Where, in this deluge, was there room in my life for a long-disregarded son of the "great" Bach?

I'm not actually sure what changed. It must have been a number of factors: a flurry of particularly excellent recordings; the perpetual desire to hear something new and truly different; maybe a keener mode of listening over time. All I know is that suddenly C. P. E. sounded absolutely fascinating, compelling, urgently expressive, and beautiful. Music is like that. You can go for years thinking that you dislike or don't care about a composer or a specific work, and then it just hits you and you wonder where it's been and how you possibly could have missed it. You have to be in the mood, or particularly receptive in some way, and you also need to take the time to listen—really listen, without preconceptions or interruptions. These opportunities are rare, and it seems that they are becoming rarer as more and more outlets for information and entertainment clamor for our attention.

One way that technology came to the rescue was through the invention of the iPod. As I'm sure many of you know, classical orchestral music, with its wide dynamic range, can be difficult to listen to through standard earbuds, especially in an outdoor environment. To hear the quiet stuff you have to turn the volume up, but you risk deafness at the climaxes. Piano music, on the other hand, reproduces particularly well, and so I started looking for repertoire I hadn't heard to death that would be fun to sample while walking outdoors. I figured that I would give C. P. E. Bach a shot. This, obviously, was not the ideal listening situation that I just mentioned above, but what I discovered was that the music couldn't be ignored or relegated to the background. It grabbed my attention and held it, even though the tunes were odd and full of what I then regarded as fussy ornamentation, and it was sometimes difficult to grasp why they had this tendency to fly off on unexpected tangents.

In this respect Bach's works were different from the music of Haydn, who I have always adored. Haydn's surprises for the most part are always explained in terms of their larger context. They often serve an audible, structural purpose. Bach's, on the other hand, remain astonishing events that come and go with disconcerting suddenness. I eventually realized that with C. P. E. the music's immediacy of effect was so important, and its rate of change so rapid, that I really could see why it was sometimes described as incoherent. It's not—far from it—but the feeling of coherence comes after the initial shock, once you get to know it, whereas in works of the Viennese school the surprises are surprising because they disrupt a formal balance that the music leads us to expect from the start. I'm not sure if that makes sense in words, but it is a very audible and, I think, accurate description of the difference.

Coincidentally, around the same time I was also really put off by a remark about Bach made by the brilliant scholar and pianist, the late Charles Rosen, in his seminal book *The Classical Style*. This is a stunning work of scholarship and essentially a paean of praise to the music of Haydn, Mozart, and Beethoven. Few writers have been able to express so intelligently just what makes their music so wonderful, and why we still love it. I had known the book since the 1970s and felt it was due for rediscovery. At one point, on page 115, Rosen makes the following statement: "C. P. E. Bach's breadth lacks grandeur just as his passion lacked wit."

Now, I ask you, what on earth does that mean? What could possibly justify such a sweeping, patently silly statement? More to the point, why is it necessary to "prove" the greatness of (in this case) Haydn at a very different composer's expense? Amid much in the book that remains wonderful, this claim didn't pass the smell test. The reason it didn't is not because Haydn is not a demonstrably greater composer than most of his contemporaries, or even than C. P. E. Bach, but because Rosen was taking Bach to task for his failure to succeed at a task he never attempted in the first place. His comment, in short, was a cheap shot. I found the unfairness galling, for some reason, and unworthy coming from an artist and scholar of Rosen's stature.

So, thanks to Apple, and my annoyance on rereading Rosen, here was music that I felt sure deserved some dedicated listening—not because I had to do it for professional reasons as a critic, but for my own personal pleasure. This is a classic case of there being no such thing as bad publicity. Trashing an artist, composer, or performer is often just as likely to attract an audience as dissuade one, and as you can see, Rosen was an exquisitely articulate trash man.

Of course, all of us critics (I hope) get into the business because we love music, but the truth is that if you take the profession at all seriously then opportunities to mix business with pleasure happen about as infrequently as they do with most jobs. Critical listening to recordings, which involves making real-time comparisons between multiple versions of the same music and explaining what specific performers do—and why it matters—may be very rewarding, but it is still work, and light years away from relaxing at home with a favorite disc of a beloved piece. With C. P. E. Bach I had a sneaking suspicion that I had hit the mother lode, and so it proved.

Mahler famously said, "The symphony must be the world, it must embrace everything." C. P. E. Bach's music, similarly, is a world, teeming with life and suitable for human habitation. What this means, practically speaking, is that there's a lot to explore, the act of listening never turns stale, and even in quantity it won't kill your enthusiasm. The fact that Bach wrote primarily instrumental music may have been bad for his reputation historically, but it's a boon now. Just imagine if he truly had followed in his father's footsteps—he did try, remember—and churned out a few hundred more church cantatas for Leipzig. Does anyone for a moment believe we would care? Telemann wrote something like a thousand. When was the last time you heard one? There is a limit to how much of that stuff we can take. J. S. Bach reached it.

So, C. P. E.'s failures, as much as his successes, made him the composer that he ultimately became. That is also the reason I think it's important to reject the snobbery of those who suggest that writing for "the public" meant an unwelcome degree of artistic compromise. Clearly it did not, even if he didn't always feel free to do as he pleased. Had he been forced as a composer to satisfy Frederick the Great, he would have been even unhappier. That much is certain. Also, there is no evidence to suggest that Bach would have done better had he been given license to write only for himself. Sure, he might have been more satisfied, but what about the listener? I firmly believe that it is precisely because he wrote for an audience, because he had to make his music sellable and earn a living, that he achieved enduring greatness. For all of his music's originality, quirkiness, seriousness, sincerity—even genius—ultimately C. P. E. Bach was still one of us, and we can hear it in every note that he wrote.

Further Reading and Discography

Much of the literature on C. P. E. Bach consists of scholarly essays intended for academic insiders. This is only to be expected given the opportunities that the recent recovery of so much of his music affords; and as I mentioned in the preface there is a lot that we don't know, and even more that remains to be explored. It is, relatively speaking, a very new field. However, there are three sources that I can recommend with enthusiasm. The first of these is Daniel Heartz's *Music in European Capitals: The Galant Style, 1720–1780* (W. W. Norton), which provides a brilliant, thorough, and very readable overview of European music during the heart of the eighteenth century, including a survey of Bach's contributions to the sonata and the concerto. The book is worth reading all by itself for anyone interested in the period.

For those who want to explore Bach's music in greater depth, David Schulenberg's *The Music of Carl Philipp Emanuel Bach* (University of Rochester Press) represents the logical next step. This is simply the most thorough, complete discussion of Bach's life and music yet published. Schulenberg is an early music specialist, an authority on the music of the Bach family, and a contributor to the new Complete Works Edition. Currently head of the music department at Wagner College on Staten Island, New York, the book can be used in tandem with a website containing additional material and audio clips of all of the music examples cited. It's a remarkable achievement, and its release was timed to coincide with the three hundredth anniversary of Bach's birth in 2014.

Two notes of caution, however: first, the book, like Heartz's, is pricey, and second, although the biographical portions are fine for the general reader, the musical analysis optimally requires at least some knowledge of theory and, better still, some practical experience playing a keyboard instrument. In any event, Schulenberg looks set to become the cornerstone of the Bach literature for many years to come.

By far the most complete and readily accessible resource, however, is the website of the Packard Humanities Institute's Complete Works Edition, which you can find at cpebach.org. Here you can browse the introductions to all of the volumes—very well written and researched—as well as explore links to additional information including a chronology of life and works, Bach's Estate Catalog, Wotquenne's complete catalog, score facsimiles, and many more items of interest. Best of all, it's free. I found it invaluable in putting together this book, and it's great just to browse and explore at your leisure. You can also purchase the scores themselves straight from the website, and the individual volumes are all beautifully printed and priced amazingly reasonably for sheet music.

Speaking of sheet music Paul Corneilson, the managing editor of the Edition, has also assembled a very useful sampler of Bach's "greatest hits," *The Essential C. P. E. Bach*, containing more than 350 pages of music in all of the media in which Bach worked, complete with user-friendly commentary on the individual works. It's available directly on the website for $50. Following music in score is certainly not necessary for most listeners (indeed, it can be a distraction), but for anyone who reads music and is curious about the actual notes, this collection makes the perfect place to start. I have also been guided by Corneilson's selection in putting together the musical samples that come with this book, so that if you do take the plunge, you will already have recordings of several of the works ready to hand.

This brings us to the subject of recordings more generally. As with everything in the record industry, the catalog of available music is in a constant state of flux. The situation with C. P. E. Bach is particularly messy in that a lot is available, but we have no idea for how long, or how easy it will be to source. There are quite a few monster collections and series on the market, and pride of place must go to Ana-Marija Markovina's twenty-six disc set of the complete music for solo keyboard (Hänssler Classic). Played on the modern piano, the performances are splendid, her interpretive decisions regarding embellishments and repeats beyond reproach, and if you prefer digital downloads, you can find these discs on iTunes in single volumes that are ideal for sampling. Markovina's performances are the ones included in the listening samples that I have chosen. Also on Hänssler, Michael Rische has recorded four discs of concertos (including Wq 23, featured here), and you can also find excellent discs of the string symphonies and violin sonatas on this same label.

I have already mentioned in several places the complete concerto edition on BIS, featuring Miklós Spányi with various period instrument ensembles. He has also undertaken a complete edition of the music for solo keyboard. These performances are a mixed bag, mostly because Spányi has a tendency to play allegros too slowly, thus sacrificing some of the music's inherent excitement and impetuosity.

Also, like so many period instrument specialists, he seems to think that the choice of instrument (and he uses many) will do at least some of his work for him, and that simply is not true. At times you get the feeling that you are listening to an experiment as opposed to a performance, and that surely was not his intention since he's a serious artist with plenty of technique and often very good ideas. Some of the recordings are exquisite (try volumes 14 and 17 in the concerto series), and he is the only source at present for the complete orchestral sonatinas and many of the concertos. Also, BIS has the happy habit of keeping its discs in print, so availability should not be a big issue.

There are Big Boxes of Bach available from several labels, including DG Achiv, Deutsche Harmonia Mundi, Warner Classics, Brilliant Classics, and Capriccio. All of these contain a somewhat random assortment of sonatas, concertos, symphonies, chamber music, and vocal works, and you can have a look at each and see if the selection appeals to you. As you might expect, the performances tend to be variable, but the quality is generally quite high. Boxed sets tend to come and go in the catalog rather quickly, so if you find something of interest, better to get it sooner rather than later. The German label CPO has several very good discs of concertos, chamber music, occasional choral works, and songs mostly featuring keyboardist Ludger Rémy and his group Les Amis de Philippe. Naxos also has several discs of keyboard sonatas and an excellent set of the complete flute concertos with soloist Patrick Gallois.

Finally, I want to list five superb individual discs that belong in every C. P. E. Bach collection, indeed, in every classical music collection more generally. Before making an investment in one of the large sets, you may want to start here.

1. Sonatas and Rondos. Mikhail Pletnev, piano. (Deutsche Grammophon)

This magnificent collection contains a broad selection of some of Bach's most conceptually daring pieces, starting with the Sonata in G Minor, Wq 65/17. Like Markovina, Pletnev demonstrates just how well this music adapts to the modern piano, and how beautifully it responds to true virtuoso style and expression.

2. Rondos and Fantasias. Christine Schornsheim, tangent piano. (Capriccio)

Christine Schornsheim is a period instrument specialist best known for her excellent Haydn and J. S. Bach recordings for this same label. She has chosen a program of rondos and fantasias from the *Kenner und Liebhaber* series, played on an absolutely gorgeous sounding tangent piano—sort of a clavichord on steroids. This is the kind of recital that makes the best possible case for using period instruments, as Schornsheim wrings every drop of atmosphere and color from these endlessly inventive pieces.

3. Symphony Wq 183/1; Symphony Wq 182/4; Symphony Wq 182/5; Symphony Wq 183/3; Symphony Wq 179. Orchestra of the Age of Enlightenment, Rebecca Miller, cond. (Signum)

Here are some of Bach's best symphonies played to a fare-thee-well by an excellent period instrument orchestra under the lively and sympathetic leadership of Rebecca Miller. The disc is a joy from start to finish, and a perfect Bach symphony sampler.

4. Magnificat, Wq 215; *Heilig ist Gott*, Wq 217; Symphony in D Major Wq 183/1. Akademie für Alte Musik Berlin; RIAS-Kammerchor Harmonia Mundi, Hans-Christoph Rademann, cond. (Harmonia Mundi)

Most "concept" albums fail because the music doesn't fit the concept. This one succeeds because it offers the second half of an actual concert given by Bach, one that included choral works by Handel and his father on the first half. We don't actually know which symphony he offered, but this one, possibly his most famous, fits the bill nicely. The Magnificat and the *Heilig* are two of Bach's supreme vocal masterpieces, and they are fabulously played and sung by the forces gathered together here.

5. Sonata in A Minor, Wq 49/1; 12 Variations on "Les Folies d'Espagne"; Sonata in G Minor, Wq 65/17; Fantasie in F-sharp Minor, Wq 67; Rondo in C Minor, Wq 59/4; Sonata in E Minor, Wq 59/1; Fantasia in C Major, Wq 61/6. Andreas Staier, harpsichord. (Deutsche Harmonia Mundi)

Andreas Staier is one of the outstanding keyboard players of our time. Most recently he has made a very good set of the Six Keyboard Concertos, Wq 43 for the other Harmonia Mundi label (France), and if you're looking for a single disc collection of solo keyboard works played on a really zingy, bright-toned harpsichord in contrast with a mellower but equally characterful fortepiano, this is the disc to get. It includes Wq 65/17, which means you can compare it to Pletnev on the piano, and I have to say that in this case I think the harpsichord wins. This disc is also included in the Deutsche Harmonia Mundi boxed set mentioned above.

Notes

Chapter One

1 C. P. E. Bach, *Essay on the True Art of Playing Keyboard Instruments*, trans. William J. Mitchel (New York: W. W. Norton, 1949), 147.
2 Ibid., 79.
3 Ibid., 173.
4 Ernest Eugene Helm, *Music at the Court of Frederick the Great* (Norman: University of Oklahoma Press, 1960), 173.

Chapter Two

5 C. P. E . Bach, *Autobiography*, trans. Jost Hermand and James Steakley, in *Writings of German Composers* by Hermand and Steakley (New York: Continuum, 1984), 39.
6 C. P. E. Bach, *Essay on the True Art of Playing Keyboard Instruments*, trans. William J. Mitchel (Norton: New York, 1949), 152.
7 Ibid., 153.
8 Stephen L. Clark, *The Letters of C. P. E. Bach* (Oxford: Clarendon Press, 1997), 213.
9 Bach, *Autobiography*, 38–39.
10 C. P. E. Bach, *Six Keyboard Sonatas with Varied Reprises*, ed. Eiji Hashimoto (New York, G. Schirmer, Inc., 1988).
11 Bach, *Essay*, 81.

Chapter Five

12 Quoted in C. P. E. Bach, *Orchester-Sinfonien mit zwölf obligaten Stimmen*, ed., David Kidger, The Complete Works III, vol. 3 (Los Altos: Packard Humanities Institute, 2005), xv.

Chapter Six

13 Stephen L. Clark, *The Letters of C. P. E. Bach* (Oxford: Clarendon Press, 1997), 41–42.
14 Author's translation.

15 C. P. E. Bach: *Gellert Songs*, ed. Darell M. Berg, The Complete Works VI, vol. 1 (Los Altos: Packard Humanities Institute, 2009), xviii.
16 C. P. E. Bach: *Gellert Songs*, ed. Anja Morgenstern, The Complete Works VI, vol. 2 (Los Altos: Packard Humanities Institute, 2009), xxiv.
17 Clark, *Letters*, 213.
18 Ibid., 270.

Chapter Seven

19 C. P. E. Bach, *Autobiography*, trans. Jost Hermand and James Steakley, in *Writings of German Composers* by Hermand and Steakley (New York: Continuum, 1984), p. 39.

Chapter Eight

20 C. P. E. Bach, *Autobiography*, trans. Jost Hermand and James Steakley, in *Writings of German Composers* by Hermand and Steakley (New York: Continuum, 1984), p. 39.
21 C. P. E. Bach: *Trio Sonatas II*, The Complete Works II, vol. 2.2, ed. Christoph Wolff (Los Altos: Packard Humanities Institute, 2011), p. 31.
22 Ibid., 32.

Chapter Nine

23 Stephen L. Clark, *The Letters of C. P. E. Bach* (Oxford: Clarendon Press, 1997), 279.

CD Track Listing

1. Concerto in D Minor, Wq 23: Allegro (8:14)
   Michael Rische, piano
   Leipzig Kammerorchester, Morten Schuldt-Jensen (cond.)
   hänssler CLASSIC 98.639

2. Concerto in D Minor, Wq 23: Poco andante (6:26)
   Michael Rische, piano
   Leipzig Kammerorchester, Morten Schuldt-Jensen (cond.)
   hänssler CLASSIC 98.639

3. Concerto in D Minor, Wq 23: Allegro assai (6:43)
   Michael Rische, piano
   Leipzig Kammerorchester, Morten Schuldt-Jensen (cond.)
   hänssler CLASSIC 98.639

4. Symphony in C Major, Wq 182 No. 3: Allegro assai (2:45)
   Stuttgarter Kammerorchester, Wolfram Christ (cond.)
   hänssler CLASSIC 98.637

5. Symphony in C Major, Wq 182 No. 3: Adagio (3:17)
   Stuttgarter Kammerorchester, Wolfram Christ (cond.)
   hänssler CLASSIC 98.637

6. Symphony in C Major, Wq 182 No. 3: Allegretto (5:37)
   Stuttgarter Kammerorchester, Wolfram Christ (cond.)
   hänssler CLASSIC 98.637

7. Sonata in C Minor, Wq 50 No. 6: Allegro moderato (6:43)
   Ana-Marija Markovina, piano
   hänssler CLASSIC 98.003

8. Solfeggio in C Minor Wq 117 No. 2: Prestissimo (0:58)
Ana-Marija Markovina, piano
hänssler CLASSIC 98.003

9. L'Aly Rupalich Wq 117 No. 27: Allegro assai (2:40)
Ana-Marija Markovina, piano
hänssler CLASSIC 98.003

10. Sonata in F Minor Wq 57 No. 6: Allegro assai (4:30)
Ana-Marija Markovina, piano
hänssler CLASSIC 98.003

11. Sonata in F Minor Wq 57 No. 6: Andante (4:28)
Ana-Marija Markovina, piano
hänssler CLASSIC 98.003

12. Sonata in F Minor Wq 57 No. 6: Andantino grazioso (5:00)
Ana-Marija Markovina, piano
hänssler CLASSIC 98.

13. Rondo in B-flat Major Wq 58 No. 5: Allegro (5:39)
Ana-Marija Markovina, piano
hänssler CLASSIC 98.003

14. Fantasia in F-sharp Minor Wq 67: Adagio "C. P. E. Bach's Feelings" (12:24)
Ana-Marija Markovina, piano
hänssler CLASSIC 98.003

Total Disc: 75:24